What's Next?

Timely Tips on Aging

Suanne Ferguson

Copyright © 2023 Suanne Ferguson

All rights reserved

ISBN: 9798862590180

Dedication

I dedidcate this book to my family. You've lived it with me one step at a time. Secondly, I dedicate this book to my students, both young and old. I may have trained you in the disciplines of dance or dance/fitness, but you have been my training ground.

Acknowledgements

Though this book has not been professionally edited, I want to thank those who have helped me edit; my son, Bill, my grandchildren, Christian (Kit) and Katherine, and friends, Rosemary and Larry. All of them helped to shape the book.

Table of Contents

Introduction: 5

Chapter One: What Fans the Flames of Your Inner Fire? 3   13

Timely Tip #1 Examine and renew your purpose

Chapter Two: Expect Change   25

Timely Tip #2 Don't waste emotional energy clinging to the past…be positive and move on

Chapter Three: Why Ballet?   33

Timely Tip #3 Take seriously the life-lesson ballet training provides

Chapter Four: A Life-Time Body   43

Timely Tip #4 Resistance builds strength

Chapter Five: The Path to Balance   58

Timely Tip #5 Sitting does not help balance

Chapter Six: Movement, Memory,, and Your Aging Mind   68

Timely Tip #6.Dancing makes you smarter

Chapter Seven: Your Spirit BurnsWithin.   84

Timely Tip #7 This could be your best season

Chapter Eight: Where Does Your Heart Lie?   102

Timely Tip #8 *Come now and listen to your heart*

Chapter Nine: All Creation Awaits You   117

Timely Tip #9 Value Your Connections

Chapter Ten: Celebration and Conclusion   131

Timely Tip #10 Make every day a Celebration Day

Appendix: 145

Resources: 153

Introduction

The secret to aging well lies in choosing your dance of life.

Are you moving on? Or, are you standing still? Of course, the answer is you are moving on because we are all moving on. We don't have a choice about that, but we do have a choice about how we're moving.

Are you marking time? Or, do you march to the beat? Do you tip toe cautiously through life or are you willing to move boldly like a Cha-Cha? About twenty years ago, I was tip toeing somewhat cautiously through life, being pushed along by the whims of others, hesitant and fearful, and then I learned to Cha-cha and it made all the difference. As I learned this dance, I began to understand how to move boldly and with purpose. I began to see that the concept could be a metaphor for living well.

My favorite poet, Mary Oliver, asks the question, "What are you doing with this one wild and precious life you have?" You see, life is a dance ... let's create our own tempo.

Aging is a hot topic today. People are living longer and seeking ways to do it well. Many of the books on aging are scientific books revealing the recent research done on gerontology. While this one contains some research, one might call this book an auto-biographical sketch of aging. I use the word sketch because it is imperfect, not professionally edited, but full of content that I want to share. At eighty-seven years of age, I now reflect to see just how I got where I am—a teacher, dancer, writer and storyteller whose mission is to help to transform lives (including my own)—one step at a time. No matter where you are in the aging process, I suggest that you give some thought to how you are aging, because without a doubt, we are all aging. We have little choice of how or when our life on earth will end, but we can choose to live well. You may think that your genes determine your longevity, but the truth is, genetics account for a maximum of 30 percent of your life expectancy. The rest comes from your behaviors, attitudes, environment, choices, and aa lot of prayer.

This poem by Brother Ramos, found on a greeting card years ago, reveals something innate to my being. It is part of my story.

"in me

something scary and wonderful

is always turning stiffness into a dance...

it is the fire of life

The fire of life—that flame burns in each and every one of us—is that flame that turns stiffness into a dance. Dance is my indigenous language, and it is also your indigenous language. It is the movement of the Spirit within us. Though we may have forgotten our dance, the language of movement is learned long before the spoken or written word. We are born dancers. Certainly, from the beginning of life, the young instinctively move. Unborn babies kick, punch, and roll in the womb. Infants stretch and squeeze tiny muscles, exploring with movement. Children wiggle, bounce, touch, and respond to the world, through movement. We inherently express ourselves, our deepest selves through movement.

Early in life, movement is natural—not self-conscious. However, we are soon encouraged to be still. As our need to move and dance is stifled we become restricted, inhibited, and stiff. The further we move from natural movement, the stiffer we become. Our bodies are made for movement, not for rigidity. When we find it difficult to move fluidly, we find it difficult to be fully engaged in life. Unfortunately, as we age, we allow stiffness to become a part of what we expect in life. A focus on how we move could change that. A focus on dance could actually expand and extend our lives. Movement/Dance brings abstract concepts to life, extending them, and giving them reality. It requires both discipline and direction while it incorporates imagination and joy. It engages the whole person—body, mind, and spirit.

Look for the dancer in yourself. The dance of life expresses itself in every movement we make. As we age, we must welcome every obstacle to movement as an opportunity to become a better dancer. Any human that can move at all can create new patterns of sensing and responding. It is possible to invite the neural network of our bodily self to create new connections. There is a dancer in each of us, and a dance in everything we do. These dances connect us to the Spirit within. While our movements, our "dances", connect us to Spirit, our stories connect us to one another. At the same time, they connect us to the Divine. Tell me a story and tell it again so that I may truly understand. We are searching for a part of ourselves, an unknown truth—a wider truth that reconnects us to our source. Dance me a story and I will be energized, renewed, and fully engaged. By dancing our stories, we engage in a deep practice of faith that leads us toward wholeness/holiness. If you are not quite ready to dance your story, share it in whatever way you can. Our stories connect us.

"For you created my inmost being. You knit me together in my mother's womb. I praise you because I am fearfully and wonderfully made."   Psalms 139: 13-14

Whether we call them affinities, attractions, spontaneities, intelligences, or aptitudes, we notice that these innate knowings contribute to our personal creation stories. They connect to our compassion, to our longevity, to our happiness, and to our personal mission in the Universe. We often tell these stories through our creativity. As we create, we give form, order, style, interpretation, and arrangement to matter, we make the connections that link us to all others in the web of life. Enthusiasm for story comes from a deep place in the psyche of each individual. We seek stories that will help to unlock the mysteriousness of our lives. Our stories can even help to heal the wounds of past mysteries.

In stories we find our personal voice and in stories we are provided images of who we are and what we are meant to do. When we share a story, hear a story, or dance a story, we are made more alive, more human, more courageous, more compassionate, even more loving. We discover that the universe has meaning, and that our lives are not irrelevant—that what we choose to do or say does matter.

The Sufi poet Rumi says:

"But don't be satisfied with poems and stories of how things have gone with others. Unfold your own myth without complicated explanation, so everyone will understand…."

You unfold your own myth with your creativity. Find your story and unfold your myth. Your own myth, your own story will help you grow into wisdom, wholeness, and healing.

This book contains parts of my story written to encourage its readers to choose life, to accept that aging is inevitable, but boredom, rigidity, hopelessness, and sadness are not.

This story is the result of twenty-five years of taking charge, of making choices. It is still a work in progress. If we don't make choices as we age, we find that others are quick to make them for us, and then we are simply victims of the choices of others. It is not that making our own choices makes it all smooth sailing. Quite the contrary, there are definite ups and downs with the choices we make. Yet, there is a sense of freshness, of newness, and of hope. as we choose life. All of these things are part of youth—and they can be a part of aging, too.

In the video documentary, "Keep Dancing," Marge Champion, now in her nineties, reminds us to live each decade for what it brings, not for what it takes away. My sixties were a time of refreshing, creating newness in my life. My seventies were a time of determination to stay well, healthy and independent. I purchased a home, started a new career as a dance fitness instructor for seniors, and continued honing my skills as a ballet teacher. Now, still in my eighties, I do not know exactly what this decade will bring. So far, my eighties have brought interesting challenges. They started out with a bout of AFib, a few months later a broken shoulder, then came a knee replacement surgery and recovery, and then six months later, a fall that resulted in a broken hip.

While I was still striving to recover from the results of the broken hip, something came that was totally unexpected—a pandemic that would change everyone's life. I became part of a large group of people known as "the most vulnerable." For weeks I struggled with being told that I must stay at home for my safety and the safety of others. I learned new technical skills like how to teach, even dance, by using Zoom. I taught my last (as far as I know) ballet class on Zoom. In fact, my lengthy career as a ballet teacher may have come to end.   Everything was uncertain. The pandemic took over all our lives. We had time on our hands —perhaps time to finish writing a book. I moved forward, finished this book and self-published it as "Take Charge of You Aging," and then, everything changed. I retired. And I moved into Senior Adult Housing, Episcopal Place. After being here almost a year, I decided that the book needs to be updated. This is Version Two…"What's Next?"

Soon after making that decision, I realized that my macular degeneration was progressing rapidly. My left eye was almost totally blind, but my right eye was seeing 20/20. Daily living, reading, even driving, were no problem. Now, six months later, I have had to give up driving, and reading has become more and more difficult. The title of "What's Next?' seems even more appropriate.

Together we will explore aging using new science and some new concepts, and my experience. Sharing some tips I've learned along the way, we will focus on movement/dance and our stories. We will look at body, mind. and spirit. Then, we will celebrate what we have learned together!

The secret to aging well lies in choosing your dance of life.

Chapter One
What Fans the Flames of Your Inner Fire?

Timely Tip#1 Examine and Renew Your Purpose

How do you live and work with meaning in purpose and how does your life benefit others?" Pondering this question, I searched back through memorabilia to remind me of my life and work, and came across a poem that I wrote years ago.

Dream on, my soul

But give me clarity of purpose

And ways of understanding

What's next? And then…

What then… what's next?

Open doors with wisdom

And clear the path ahead.

Dream on, my soul…

At 87 years of age, my soul is still dreaming. I ask the same question because it is still relevant. "How do you live and work with meaning in purpose, and how does your life benefit others?" The question is as important to me today as has been all my life. Is what I do purposeful, and does it bring meaning to my life, and to the lives of others? I reflect on an earlier part of life when my purpose was clear. Reflecting helps to renew, and perhaps, to redirect.

Flashback to 2003

My soul is touched this morning, Mother's Day, as I watch my daughter, Cindy and her two children, Kit—six years old, and Katherine—three years old, dance in worship. As they lift their hands in praise of the goodness of God, everyone seems to understand. My forty-four year old son, sitting in the pew behind me, sheds tears as he watches his sister and her children. He, too, is touched. Worshiping God through dance has long been important to our family. Dance has a powerful way of speaking to the hearts of people.

This will be a busy work-filled, soul-filled week. Cindy and I are working with Kit, and his first grade class on a multi-media benefit for the rainforest. We are in charge of the dances...will the children ever remember all their dances, songs, and their play parts? We are expecting a lot. These are, after all, first graders. They will have their uncooperative moments, they will have their forgetful moments, but in the end, they will remember. Even more important, the children's attitudes about the Earth, their part in saving and healing it, will be charged with new energy. Will it wear off on their parents who pay a few dollars to benefit the rainforest and come to see their children perform? Some will understand and may be motivated to do more. Mrs. Beasley, Kit's teacher, says, "It is the only way that change will happen." I am grateful for the Mrs. Beasleys of the world. Now Kit, is 28. He finished his Masters Degree at Georgia Tech working. on designing a car that uses less fuel. He continues to care for the Earth and its sustainability. Does his work have anything at all to do with Mrs. Beasley's rainforest project? I have to think that, indeed it does. He may not even remember the project, but that is unimportant. Experiences make an imprint on our deep understandings.

David Suzuki ends his book, *The Sacred Balance*, with these thoughts:

There is joy in the companionship of others working to make a difference for future generations, and there is hope. Each of us has the ability to act powerfully for change; together we can regain that ancient and sustaining harmony, in which human needs and the needs of all our companions on the planet are held in balance with the sacred, self-renewing processes of the Earth.

Quickly, on from the rehearsal at the elementary school to the studio. I have statements to print and sponsorships to pursue. There is also the Chamber of Commerce meeting this week. We must have resources to continue our work. Oh yes, payroll is due this week, too. My official business card reads, Suanne Ferguson, Birmingham Ballet, Marketing and Administration. I have another card that says, Suanne Ferguson, Dancer, Teacher, Writer, and Storyteller. Together they describe the sacred balance of my life and my work.

In the afternoons this week, I will try to tighten up the Spring Performance dances of my young students at Birmingham Ballet Academy. My Vine Fairies are doing well, and the Blue and Yellow Flower Fairies know their dances. The Undines are sloppy, and will Fire ever get its act together? The scenario of *The Unicorn* encourages children to follow their dreams, even into a mystical land where innocence and imagination turn into possibilities. It is a land where Fairy Princesses and Knights in Shining Armor are quick to help a little girl find the lost Unicorn, and where the Spirit of Light and Truth lends a helping hand to all. I think back now on that Spring Performance and recognize the importance of the little girl's dream and her searcher the lost Unicorn. Am I still that little girl?

Matthew Fox asks,

What about dreams? Where are the adults who should be paying attention to the dreams of the young and carrying this wisdom to the rest of us? Are we teaching our young people to learn from their dreams? To interpret them, trust them, and grasp their revelatory nature? To display them in drama, video, poetry, dance, and paint?

Matthew's questions validate my work.

My work as a dance teacher has long been my soul's dream, but does it have meaning in purpose, and does it benefit the world? This is a question that I have asked myself for a very long time. I have taught children to dance for seventy years. I knew from a very young age that it was what I wanted to do, what I was called to do, but I've been told that it was a rather frivolous pursuit. My parents thought of it as unimportant, and my husband often asked when I would get a "real job." In her book, *Take Your Soul to Work*, Tanis Helliwell says that "individuals motivated by their soul dreams feel called to do something, regardless of what society or others think of it." It has never been easy, and has often felt insignificant, but now, I'm beginning to recognize just what good work it is. David Suzuki quotes Ashley Montague in listing dance as one of the "psychic needs of a growing young child that must be fulfilled to ensure full development of a child's potential."

I came to Earth in January 1936, with dancing feet and the heart of a teacher. From the time I was very young, I was either dancing or teaching, or both. These days, my teaching heart keeps pumping out instructions. Students know we will move when I push that play button and the music begins. Whether my students now are eight or eighty years old, it really doesn't matter.

In the late eighties, one of my greatest joys was teaching dance to three, four, and five year old children in Birmingham's eight Housing Authority Project day care centers. I worked with each group for just twenty minutes a week, and the impact was astonishing. I will never forget my first experience in a project school. I was teaching creative movement. The teacher insisted that the children "stay in line." I wanted the children to move freely in response to my story, and the teacher insisted that the children do just as I was doing. The dynamics were interesting. After class, I explained to the teacher that I wasn't asking for the children to dance the "right" way—that I wanted to allow their creativity, their ideas. The teacher feared that I would loose control of the children. She soon found that this was not the case, or perhaps it was the case—but, in an appropriate way. They were learning self-discipline, not by force, but by fun and creativity.

Matthew Fox speaks of prophetic work:

> *All work worthy of being called spiritual and worthy of being called human is in some way prophetic work. It contributes to the growth of justice and compassion in the world; it contributes to social transformation, not for its own sake but for the sake of increasing justice. Such work is, in a real sense, God's work. By it we become co-creators with a God who is both just and compassionate, a lover of beauty who desires that it be shared by all creation.*

The work in the housing projects was truly prophetic work. It opened the children's eyes to new ways of relating to each other, and to ideas beyond their reality. One summer day as I taught a lesson on "The Night Sky," I asked the children quietly, "What happens at night?" I expected answers like I received in my classes in the suburbs like, "The stars twinkle" or "the moon comes out." To my surprise, their eyes got very big and one excited little girl said, "Somebody gets robbed." Not wanting to say that any answer was the "wrong" answer, I encouraged, "oh that's sad, but what else happens?" and received another quick answer, "The cockroaches come out!" Such was the reality of their existence. We went on with our lesson, using our imaginations to explore the movement of the stars, the comets, and the moon. It was just one small step towards transformation, one small step toward extending the boundaries of these children beyond the confines of project walls. Living and working with meaning seems so evident when I read my own episodic retelling.

As I continued to teach, first for other studio owners, then opening my own ballet school, founding a civic ballet company, and training students who went on to make careers for themselves as dancers, I often questioned myself. I questioned my dance education, my ability to be successful, and I doubted my calling. I continually felt that I should be doing something worthwhile, something that would make a real difference in the world. I had dreams of greatness, of recognition, and of approval. Even after directing the schools of two professional ballet companies, I never felt accomplished. My soul may have been satisfied, but my ego was not. Now, that I look back, to reflect on this long career, I do value what has happened over these many years, and I continue to fan the flames of that fire within.

several years ago, I was waiting in a restaurant for others to join me for dinner when a strapping teenage boy slid into the booth with me. He said, "I hope that you are who I think you are. Otherwise, I'm going to be very embarrassed." I laughed and asked him who he thought I was. I did not recognize him. He went on to say that he had been a part of my fifth grade dance group, "The Earthshakers," when I was using dance to teach science curriculum in public elementary schools. Now a senior in high school, he said, "I just want you to know that I didn't know it at the time, but you changed my life. Dancing changed my attitude about myself, about my relationships with others, and about what is important. I just want to thank-you." I will never forget that conversation. It thrills me even today—almost forty years later.

My soul still questions, what's next? Is the work I have done and am doing important and beneficial enough to survive me? Perhaps an answer to that question came to me this year. It all started with a simple post on social media. My friend, David, who had once been a student and member of my sacred dance company,The Emmanuel Dance Company, posted a comment that drew a response from

Scott. I answered Scott, "is this the Scoot who was once an Emmanuel Dancer?" He answered, "Once an Emmanuel Dancer, always an Emmanuel Dancer." That prompted a series of remarkable events.

The Emmanuel Dance Company was a group that I founded and directed. Early in the eighties we toured the United State performing at workshops and churches across the country, from Alabama to Massachusetts to Ohio to Colorado and back to Alabama… over 7,000 miles in six weeks. There were three women and three men in the group, all college age. I was the director, choreographer, and driver. We were a close knit group, depending on each other and on God.

Following that social media post, we connected with the entire group who were living in many different parts of the country. It had been forty years since we had connected with one another. We were eager to chat with each other and then decided on a reunion in New York City. We spent three days together remembering our journey and realizing how unique and lasting our work was. The love was real, the laughter was real, the work was real, and the people that it touched were real. It has survived and it will survive. This year, we will meet again in Birmingham, AL, where it all began.

Native American songwriter, Jack Gladstone, sings of our work in this world in his song, "The Builders." The final chorus:

Through the romance, through the dance

Over rolling plains of troubled circumstance

Into the journey, we are born

Always keep your dreams alive over the storm

And may your dreams form a love that survives you.

Your children carry the love that survives you.

Indeed, my children (both my students and my own children) do carry the love that will survive me.

In my heart, I am satisfied that at least some part of my work, my purose, will survive. That's a satisfying thing to know, and at this point, I continue to be a dancer, a teacher, a writer, and a storyteller.My church and my living situation offer opportunities to do just that.

At First Christian Church, I am a part of dance in worship, I still dance myself occasionally, and I encourage dance for people of all ages by working with the children and with multigenerational groups. Dance is an integral part of my search to be closer to God.

I started dancing at Episcopal Place, where I live, about a week after I moved in. There have been many opportunities here to both dance and to teach Dance Fitness.

All of these opportunities give me new ways to fan the flames of my inner fire. They challenge me, encourage me, and give me purpose. I'll talk about them more as we move on through my story.

Timely Tip#1 Examine and Renew Your Purpose

Chapter Two
Expect Change

Timely Tip # Don't waste time clinging to things of the past… move on and enjoy life

Lifestyle interruptions and changes

Life is all about change, and as we age those changes seem to become magnified and more difficult, especially if they are caused by health issues of any kind. We'll talk about health issues later, but I will start with lifestyle changes. These changes are not only magnified and more challenging, they may also be the most rewarding and revitalizing. Sometimes we move through life on a path of familiar repetition. We do what we know best. When we tackle a lifestyle change we are challenged to take another path, and then, maybe another. This can seem overwhelming, or it can be exciting. Sometimes we are called to make a lifestyle change when we least expect it.

My son, Bill, found his calling during an abrupt lifestyle change. He lost his job selling computer equipment, and then discovered that he had an extraordinary ability to learn new computer programs and to teach them to others. Teaching has become his passion. His technical skills and creative skills meet when he teaches both his Sunday School class, and Computer programs. If not for the abrupt change in his life, he might have missed this calling (at least for awhile).

When the pandemic provoked the closing of the ballet studio and company that my daughter, Cindy, had directed for more than 30 tees, she discovered latent skills as a sculptor. Even in her first year, her work is amazing. I told her that sculpting must be in her soul. A lifestyle change gave it a chance to come to the surface. In what could have been a devastating time of her life, new life came forth.

Well known author, Martha Beck, likens the whole process of change to that of Metamorphosis. In an article called "Growing Wings" she talks about this transformation.

She speaks of the first phase as one of dissolving and describes this stage as the scariest as we lose our identity and are left "temporarily formless." In fact, dissolving may feel like death, but you will get through it by focusing on whatever is happening right now (the unfolding events). "Dissolving isn't something you do; it's something that happens to you." You just have to relax and trust the process. You have to let go.

She describes the second phase in this way. "This is when the part of you that knows your destiny, the imago in your psyche, will begin giving you instructions about how to reorganize the remnants of your old identity into something altogether different." Your mind begins to make images of the life you are about to create. You may even develop interests and traits that your old self didn't have—you are transforming, becoming new. Daydream to develop a clearer picture of your goals and desires. You will probably go from daydreaming to creating actual plans. You might begin to gather information about how you can create them.

You are energized now toward making these dreams and goals come true, and you enter a third phase that emerges. "You'll feel motivated to do real, physical things to build a new life. And then... (drum roll, please)... you'll fail. Repeatedly. Re-forming your life, like anything new, complex and important, inevitably brings up problems you didn't expect." Even when you seem to be failing, it is important to continue to work toward your dreams. Make new and improved plans until they work.

And then rejoice in the last phase, the phase of Flying. This is when your new identity is fully formed and you are able to fly. "Don't attribute your happiness to your new identity; security lies in knowing how to deal with metamorphosis, whenever it occurs. Just remember that what the caterpillar calls the end of the work, the master calls a butterfly."

Part of aging is learning to cope with and thrive through each and every change. We often choose our changes in an effort to live the best life possible. If we don't make important decisions for ourselves because we are afraid that they might leave us in unknown territory, or that we might fail, we will lose opportunities to grow. And, even in the midst of our very best choices, unexpected change may appear. We are challenged then, to make new decisions. We age far less quickly with the choices and changes we enter with thought and decision. It is a matter of moving forward with confidence. You arrived here on earth with a journey ahead of you and the power to affect that journey.

Do not be afraid to redirect and discover what is really important to you. Let go of the parts of your life that are holding you back, and move toward those that you love. Yes, we can let life just happen leaving us feeling like a victim, or we can choose life. That is not to say that we can control life, because we can't—there is a much greater Divine Love handling that. We can make choices for ourselves that determine our path toward a rich and fulfilling journey.

You have brains in your head. You have feet in your shoes. You can steer yourself any direction you choose. You're on your own. And you know what you know. And YOU are the one who'll decide where to go... Dr. Seuss "Oh The Places You'll Go"

At sixty-one years of age, I made an abrupt change in my lifestyle. I made the choice to become single, and I began my new life doing exactly what I had been doing—teaching ballet. It was what I knew best, and what I knew could support me. My dreams and my vision had changed though. First, I went back to school. After getting my Master's Degree, I began to feel very entrepreneurial. I stepped outside the dance studio to create a new business called **Wisdom Stories**. I hired a Marketing Consultant, and established a motivational speaking and consulting business offering unique, inspiring, and informative steps toward creating a better life, and better business practices. I designed a program called ***Tempo!***™ focusing in a new way on five essential disciplines of the ballet barre. I marketed this program to businesses in the Birmingham area as an instrument for corporate change. After a couple of really good experiences with innovative companies, I discovered that corporations, as a whole, are not ready to step too far "out of the box." What did ballet have to do with business? I soon realized that I was not going to be able to support myself as I sought to develop and grow this business, and this interruption resulted in a new focus. I shifted the same my age group and beyond, to change, and to become more fit and more confident. *Wisdom Stories* became Moving Toward Health. My mission was to "empower and transform lives one step at a time."

My bio in those years, read, Suanne Ferguson is a teacher, writer, dancer, and storyteller, empowering and transforming lives by sharing the disciplines of dance training.

To incapsulate the next fifteen years, I taught my signature fitness program for seniors, ***Tempo!™***, in retirement centers and churches in Jefferson and Shelby Counties. Later I became licensed in ZUMBA® and ZUMBA® Gold, offering this international fitness system in a variety of settings. With Cynthia Alicea, I became Co-Director of Ageless Adventures in Movement, offering workshops across the country in Creative Movement for Older Adults, and out of that grew the AAIM Dance Ensemble, a performance group of seniors exploring, through dance, the global issues of aging. And then, again, I added teaching ballet to children.

I wrapped the motivational talk, **Movin' On**, into my senior fitness business. That first year, I spoke at more than 100 different venues serving seniors—churches, retirement homes, and senior centers. I suggested we move boldly like a Cha Cha. This is definitely a delightful way to move through life. Life and purpose create a dance. We create our own tempo—the pace and the pulse of the dance—the energy and passion with which we engage in our purpose.In other words, the pace and pulse of our movement depends on the unfolding events in our environment. I like the concept of unfolding events because the events of our lives do seem to unfold in front of us, not revealing themselves until we are directly on top of them.

Tempo!™ (the class includes warmup, strength training, flexibility and relaxation) and ZUMBA® Gold, (aerobic dancing) kept me very busy and purposeful for many years. In both classes, we begin by moving.., dancing. Next, we begin to feel the rhythm of the dance. The dance enters our body and mind, and we suddenly know without hesitation the right steps, and the right direction to go. That is when we really start to enjoy the dance. And then, we choose the next dance, the next rhythm, and we just keep moving on. Missteps along the way don't matter either. They are short-lived and temporary.

And then, suddenly, I was eighty-six. I retired from teaching, moved into Senior Adult Housing. I made changes that I never thought I would make. For the past year, I have struggled through the "dissolving process" that Martha Beck talked about. And, I am emerging. I will share those changes as I rewrite parts of this book. Strangely enough, as I rewrite, I am learning anew.

Timely Tip #2 Don't waste emotional energy clinging to the past…be positive and move on and enjoy life

ChapterThree
Why Ballet?

Timely Tip #3 Take Seriously the life-lessons learned from the ballet barre

Discipline and training lead to possibilities

My mission lies in combining the user of story with the e energy of dance to empower the creativity that lies within. When one thinks and trains like a dancer, nothing is impossible. As a ballet teacher for seventy years, I appreciate the discipline and the training of the ballet dancer. The small child (usually seven or eight years old), just beginning training, spends much of the class at the bae. This develops discipline, balance, flexibility, control, and knowledge of the movement vocabulary of ballet. As the dancer progresses, all of the aspects of the barre are brought to the center of the room and the movement vocabulary expands. No matter how accomplished the dancer becomes, the barre work is the beginning of every class. Exercises are in the same order as they were in the early years, and they are more complex and challenging.It has been said, "If you miss one day at the barre you notice it. If you miss two days at the barre , the instructor notices. If you miss three days at the barre,, the audience notices. And, if you miss four days at the barre, everyone notices," The training of a dancer takes at least eight years. The eight to twelve year old dancers became my speciality. I love the process of early training.

After years and years of training young ballet dancers, I began to notice that ballet training, especially the barre, holds many metaphors that relate to life itself. I began to see that these metaphors could be useful in many different areas. Both my business model called The Ballet of Business. ,and the senior dance fitness program called *Tempo!* use the ballet barre as my inspiration.

As we choose to move boldly and begin to train like a dancer, we will want to consider certain basic dance and life/work disciplines. The ballet barre will serve as a guide.

Bend: encourage flexibility - *Plie'...bending the knees*

Bending encourages creates flexibility. A dancer holds his/her body erect and bends the turned out knees It is the first exercise at the barre. At the very bottom of the move, the dancer presses back up to standing. Combining porte de bras, the use of the arms often combined with a bend ing of the body, with the plie' combination leads to bending the entire body in a variety of directions. Flexibility is the goal. In life, flexibility is crucial.

Perhaps the first thing we must do is to to be ready to bend. Are you "stove-up" with arthritis that makes it hard to bend anything in your body? Perhaps, an unbending mind and unbending spirt accompanies the stiffness we feel in our bodies. As we slowly begin to bend our bodies, we may find a change. In attitude at the same time.

A little reed bends to the force of the wind and stands upright again when the storm has passed. Are you ready to do the same when the storms of life come your way? I visited Charleston, S.C. long ago and marvel at the Live Oak trees with their massive trunks and far reaching branches. They looked strong and sturdy, but not long after, a hurricane hit and many of the Live Oak trees were simply uprooted. They could not bend in the wind.

Sometimes our minds are inflexible. Are you stuck in a mind-set? Perhaps, you've been doing the same thing for some time now. Your world is getting smaller and smaller. In your darkest moments, you feel trapped. Perhaps, you have just stopped seeing the possibilities. Or, it might be that you have an unbending attitude.

Try a bending attitude—an attitude that allows you to move in directions you may never have moved before. Allow yourself to bend boldly knowing that you are creating a new shape and a new space for yourself. Allow yourself to dance! Growing is all about the twists and turns. It is about bending to find new adventure in your life. That sense of adventure is really about waking up every day, not with a sense of the sameness trap, but with a sense of possibility. Are you willing to bend your body, mind and spirit?

Stretch: extend- *Tendu…stretching the feet*

The second exercise of the barre is tendu, the stretch of the foot. It is the goal of every dancer to have beautifully stretched feet. What stretching goals might we have for ourselves?

What stands in the way of your reaching, stretching, and growing? Have you ever thought, "I'm too old to do that?" We are stifled by that thought. Through stretching our minds, we can envision a bigger picture. We work to stretch into that picture, to risk extending into what we envision. Stretching is a step out of your comfort zone toward personal growth. We like our comfort zones. As we age, we sink deeper and deeper into comfort. Why risk trying something new, when we are comfortable with sameness?

We have to be ready to stretch into a new picture, to risk moving into a picture that we envision. Are you willing to risk enough to stretch into that vision? Are you willing to move out of your comfort zone, to extend your range of motion? Stretching is the first step toward expanding your life and reaching toward any kind of personal growth.

A wise person once said to me, "We are either growing or we are decaying. Decaying doesn't sound very appealing to me. My ballet teacher said, "Stretch to the edge of pain." Notice that he said to go the edge, not into pain. Our goal is personal growth.

"To the edge," he said. "No, no, not to the edge." "To the edge," he said. "No, no not to the edge." Then she stepped to the edge and she flew. What is challenging you to the edge? Will you dare to fly? Will you leave your comfort zone?

Disengage: empower yourself and others - *Dégagé…disengage the stretching foot from the floor*

In a dégagé, the dancers foot stretches so much that it actually leaves the floor. The foot reaches beyond the limits of the floor. The word mean disengage.

To empower ourselves and others we must **let go** By stepping out of the way, we enhance the opportunities for the success of others. By stepping out of our own way, we empower ourselves.

Egyptian proverb: *The marksman hitteth the mark partly by pulling, partly by letting go.*

What is keeping you from going a new direction? Could you let go of whatever it is that is holding you back?

It is not easy to let go. As in the exercise for the dancer, it requires control, balance, antability. Likewise in life, letting go is not easy. At no time in life do we find ourselves challenged to let go more than as we reach the "older adult" category. Some must let go of homes that they have known for most of their lives. Some have to let go of physical abilities like eye sight, and hearing, and moving easily. Some must give up the independence that driving a car gives them. These are frustrating issues of letting go and they definitely require choosing a new direction. We might be challenged to let go, but we don't have to let that define us. In our letting go, we must find balance and stability.

Here is another perspective on letting go. What could we choose to let go of that would actually benefit us? I think first, that I could let go of a preconceived idea of what I can and cannot do. It is a challenge to keep trying to surpass what I thought I could do. I am challenged to keep growing, to keep stretching, to go beyond the self-imposed chains that would hold me back.

Would it also help to let go of resentments, regrets, fears, habits, and attitudes that limit us? Ponder this question and see where it leads you.

Circle: embrace creativity and collaboration - *Rond djambe…circle of the leg*

In a ronde de jamb, the dancer holds the body still and circles the leg in the hip socket. Our joints are uniquely able to circle in this way. Our minds can also think in a more circular way. Unlike narrow linear thinking and linear movement, circular thinking is creative. Circular movement allows us to connect with others and to create continuity of effort. Energize with others by collaboration.

Many think in a linear way—in other words, thinking in a straight line, or in a ladder like way. Linear thinking encourages one to think "this is right and that is wrong." On the other hand a circular type of thinking is creative thinking. There is no right or wrong, just endless possibilities. Circles get things moving. Just as a wheel allows the car to move, circular thinking allows us to move with endless possibility. With a flat tire, the car goes nowhere—when it is round again, movement can begin.

When we circle around something (an item or an idea), we see it from different perspectives. What could a different perspective mean to you?

Kick: energize passion - *grand battement, a large* *kick in any direction*

Letting go in a big way is a grand battement. The dancers pushes right through the dégagé and lets the leg fly upward. This movement involves a great release of energy and intensity.

In life that great release of energy and intensity could be described as passion. With all the energy of a high kick—be passionate. Passion is energy from the inside—out. Your enthusiasm generates action allowing you to energize, empower, and excel.

Be bold! Be passionate about something—anything. Be excited about the changes you are making. Be a little wild. Let your ideas fly. Your passion will energize you.

Timely Tip #3 Take seriously the life-lessons learned from the ballet barre

Chapter Four
A Life-Time Body

Timely Tip #4 Resistance builds strength

The Road to Physical Freedom

I expect my body to last a life-time, however long that lifetime. In order for it to do that, I need to take charge of what I do with this aging body to prevent what many have come to know as the "normal effects of aging." We can actually prevent a great deal of the wear and tear that many people experience. Lifting weights, and other forms of resistance training can reverse some of the signs of aging.

In this section we will look at the ways in that strength training does. indeed, make us stronger. First we will look at some of science of aging that is inevitable. We can't prevent sarcopenia, the loss of muscle fiber.

Sarcopenia is a scary sounding word, and a scary condition. The term is derived from Greek root words, sarx (flesh), and penia (loss). Literally, we begin to lose our flesh —our muscle mass. Along with the corresponding gain of fat mass and many natural biochemical modifications, if we do not take charge, we will experience serious functional and metabolic outcomes that negatively influence our quality of life. Sarcopenia typically arises during the fourth decade of life, accelerates after the age of 50, and may advance more rapidly after the approximate age of seventy-five.

You might want to visit the website called sarcopenia.com. At sarcopenia.com, they state that they "seek to bring the role of skeletal muscle center stage, since we believe that it's not just about living longer, but about the quality of life that we lead—a life where 'strength equals freedom."

The expression, one thing leads to another, is so true with the advent of sarcopenia in our forties. Imagine a cascading effect toward all the symptoms of aging. Less muscle mass and strength leads to faster fatigue, and to the risk of falling. The fatigue leads to less physical activity, a more sedentary lifestyle, and even a greater risk and fear of falling. Less activity also results in fat gain and obesity. The weight we gain contributes to glucose intolerance, type II diabetes, and a condition called metabolic syndrome. This syndrome can then cause hypertension (high blood pressure) and increasing risk for cardiovascular disease. The end-state of sarcopenia is death.

Some say to me, "Well, we're all going to die one way or another." Of course, that is true. However, along the way, we have the ability to make some choices that will improve our *quality of life* as long as we are living.

There are adequate studies available to show that resistance training has proven that elderly people need not live out their days stooped over and shuffling about. It is also clear that sarcopenia is accelerated with a lack of physical activity, especially the lack of overload to the muscle, as in resistance exercise. Not only has adopting a resistance training regimen early in middle age been proven to reduce the appearance of sarcopenia later in life, but weight training regimens undertaken by the elderly have been shown to actually reverse sarcopenia by redeveloping muscle mass.

The good news is that we are born with every muscle fiber that we will ever have. In other words, our muscle fibers develop in the womb. Our muscles grow by making changes to the already present fibers. What this means is very important to the aging adult. It simply means that even with sarcopenia present, you can still get stronger. With strength training, motor units that were previously inactive can become active, and the surviving motor units (made up of muscle fibers) can also become larger and stronger. The brain can actually increase its ability to coordinate the recruitment of individual motor units. And, even beyond that:

One of the most important adaptations to strength training is that we can overcome, or decrease, nervous inhibition to the muscles. Nervous inhibition is both psychological and physiological. In a psychological sense, confidence increases, allowing strength never before thought possible.

This really is good news. It means that you are in charge. You can decide to begin or increase your resistance training. Age, is not the issue. Sarcopenia is not the issue. The true concern is whether or not you want to become stronger and remain healthy. While you can still make the decision, it is important to do so because the day may come when you can no longer make that decision. If you do not take charge, your journey from fit to frail may be a short one.

Muscle wasting contributes radically to lives of older adults. A person who becomes incapable of the activities of daily living, such as rising unassisted from a chair, is usually institutionalized in a nursing home or an assisted living residence where he/she remains until death. Well-meaning health care providers and caregivers often make decisions that alter the lifestyles of their patients dramatically. At that point, an individual's choices are diminished significantly.

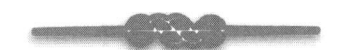

Fit to Frail

I have seen a few of my former students go from fit to frail in what seemed like overnight. When we deprive muscle fibers of working, they decide we do not need them. Alas, as I edit this writing in 2023, this chapter that I wrote years ago jumps out at me. In January 2020, I broke my hip in a fall. Then just about the time that I was about to resume "normal" activities, we were told to shelter in place, there is a pandemic—stay home. I could easily move from fit to frail. It is up to me to take charge of doing something about that.

I wrote on Facebook this morning… "I got the mile in! I'm a barrel of mixed emotions today. Walking the mile was something I could decide to do and I did…it was a take charge moment!"

Thinking of Mildred makes me smile. I met her when she was 100 years old. What a fireball! Mildred was a tiny little lady standing less than five feet tall. With a ready smile she walked the halls of her retirement center using a walker to steady her (she only used the walker because "they" told her that she had to so she would not fall). She came to exercise class twice a week, and loved the *stand to sit* exercise. She was determined to keep her legs strong, and she was strong. Then, she started complaining to the staff that her legs were tired. From my perspective, I would have worked with her to discover what else we could do to keep her legs strong, what strength training we might add. A little more variety from her persistent walking might have been just enough to keep her legs from being tired. I was not asked though, and the staff decided that she should have a wheel chair because she was at risk of falling. It took *three weeks* for Mildred to go from fit to frail—unable to walk at all. This was totally because Mildred was not able to choose for herself. This was sad to me. She was so determined to stay strong.

When I met Evelyn, she was a very active, vibrant woman in her early eighties. Her children couldn't get over how she was thriving since she had started exercising three days a week. She never missed a class, and then one night, she woke in the night with back pain and pains in her legs. The pains were severe enough that she went to her doctor. Evelyn came back to exercise class a few times after that, but said that her doctor told her that the exercise was probably too much for her with her arthritis, that she should stop our class now, and just do water exercise. I saw Evelyn a few times in the halls after that and her demeanor had totally changed. She looked sad and withdrawn, not the vibrant person I knew. She seemed to be spending more and more time just sitting—*afraid* to move. After that, I saw Evelyn regularly as I passed her room in the assisted living area. She rarely moves out of her chair and she is afraid that if she does she will fall, and she does fall often. When I encourage her to come to the seated class we do in assisted living she said, "Oh no dear. It's not good for me to move much… my arthritis you know." The time it took from very fit to very frail—less than a year.

Liona is another gutsy little (less than five feet tall) woman—busier than a hornet's nest when I met her. She proudly mentioned that she was 96 years old. (I had guessed 86.) Liona came to exercise three times a week without fail. She also went out walking regularly, and won the senior state championship at shuffle board. From 96 years old to 99, Liona was invincible. Then when she was 99, the doctor put her on a blood-thinning drug. I'm not sure of the circumstances. She didn't like it because it made her tired. She didn't have her usual energy and it was causing her stomach to bruise. Strong-minded gal that she was, she took herself off the medicine… not a smart move as it ended up (but, I understood why she did it). After she took herself off the medicine she suffered a stroke. She was back in exercise the day she got home from rehab. She was determined to get her strength back. So determined was she that she went to the therapy room by herself and got on the treadmill at 9:00 at night. Unfortunately, she fell off. Someone just happened to come near the room and found her there. She needed a few stitches in her hand and was otherwise okay. But, doctor's orders… no more treadmill. And, she was told that she must use a walker. Liona flies through the halls with her walker. She won the walking competition at the Senior Olympics (with her walker), and at 103 years of age still goes to exercise and walks every day. She's as determined as anyone I've ever seen to maintain her strong lifestyle.

One day, I had just three ladies at my assisted living fitness class—Mildred, 100 years old, Liona 103 years old, and Laura, a 68 year old lady who was having lung issues and was in a wheel chair, and, was on oxygen. At the end of class Laura was tired and Liona, who had been told that she must use a walker, said that she would push the wheelchair back to Laura's room. As I was going say, "No, let me take her," I turned my head to see Mildred doing the stand to sit exercise in front of her wheelchair. As I went to make sure that it was locked so that she would not fall, Liona took off down the hall with Laura. Then I realized that at the end of the hall, Liona would not have her walker to get back. I got Mildred back into the chair, and turned to see Liona returning to get her walker by using the hall handrail, hand over hand. Mildred and Liona were a determined pair. You'd think I could handle two ladies over 100 years old. I admired them so. Perhaps, both of them could have stayed fit much longer had they not been encouraged to stop using those muscles. Were they literally, encouraged to become frail? The fact is that frail people are easier to take care of than those who are walking the halls determined to keep on.

I tell these stories because they are real examples of people who were determined tasty strong as long as they possibly could. We must be determined to keep our strength as long as we can. Appropriate strength is extremely important as we strive to take charge of aging.

Physical Freedom

Our skeletal muscles provide us with the physical freedom we each hope to enjoy for a lifetime. They provide the strength to stand, walk, and pick things up. They provide the independence we so long to maintain.

The motor neurons are responsible for sending signals from the brain to the muscles to initiate movement. A motor unit consists of the motor neuron and all of the muscle fibers that it connects to or innervates. The loss of muscle fibers begins with the loss of motor neurons. Motor neurons will die with age resulting in a denervation of the muscle fibers within the motor unit. This denervation causes the muscle fibers to atrophy and eventually die, leading to a decrease in muscle mass. When a motor neuron dies, an adjacent motor neuron, usually a slow twitch (ST) motor neuron, may re-innervate the muscle fibers, preventing atrophy. This process is called motor unit remodeling.

There it is again—the good news that remodeling is possible. We can change the strength and size of our muscles. Yet it's this erosion called sarcopenia, and the speed at which it occurs that is directly impacting the lives of aging adults. If we choose a sedentary lifestyle, we are choosing a future of frailty and disability. Sometimes I am told, "I don't exercise anymore. I'm too old for that and besides, I deserve a rest." No one deserves or wants the disease and disruption to life that a sedentary lifestyle produces. Why does society tell us that we deserve a rest? Why do we tell each other that? Why do we tell ourselves that?

For years, I taught **Tempo!™** and Zumba® Gold at a church's "life center" that features a gym, and a fitness room with weight machines, free weights, treadmills, elliptical, and bikes. Arriving early to get set-up in the gym for class, I would find others are also arriving and gathering for activities. A few would join me in the gym for class, a dance fitness class. One or two people would head for a treadmill. Most got the dominoes and cards, and sat down in chairs that allowed their backs to curve dangerously. For three hours or more, they sat, played cards or dominoes, ate, and yes, enjoyed the company of others (that's important too). They chose not to exercise, and they made this choice together. There is a sort of camaraderie involved. In a real sense, it is a group decision to choose to sit, to choose to encourage sarcopenia. They would feel so much better if they spent that first hour in exercise together and then socialized and played games together for two hours (in well-designed chairs). In between games they could move about from time to time to chat with others.

The National Institute on Aging (NIA) reports that about 30 percent of people aged 45–64 said they engaged in regular leisure-time physical activity. Only a quarter of those ages 65–74 said they do. And while experts say people age 85 and older, can benefit from exercise, only 11 percent of that age group reported being active. At the same time, NIA noted, some older adults were contacting the Institute for guidance on kinds of exercises to do, indicating interest in becoming more active. As you and I well know, it takes more than an interest. It takes action.

Let's Get Started

The first step is to find a way to train and to be trained in some form of resistance training in a way that works for you. It is important to be consistent. It must become a part of your lifestyle, not something to do if you have time or, feel really well. I do my resistance training in two ways. Both are important to overall strength and the ability to gain and to maintain strength.

In one class of traditional strength training, we do a variety of exercises designed to get the muscles to work harder. We do many repetitions with light weights.. Most of the time we isolate a particular muscle group and work specifically to strengthen that group. We do brief cardio spurts to keep the blood flowing. This is often called traditional strength training.

In my signature *Tempo!*™ classes I lead the Dance of the Weights. The reason I call it a dance is that it is done to musing, using the music to determine the timing of lifting. Throughout the continuous movement, many muscle groups are involved in a variety of ways. This is often called functional fitness, as it leads to the ability to perform tasks of daily living. In daily living activities, we seldom isolate our muscles like we do in traditional training. Functional training can be done every day because it can involve the use of fairly light weights, (p to 5 pounds) and seldom requires fewer receptions. Class begins with about 20 minutes of dance cardio movement, the weights, and additional resistance exercise and finishes with a slow stretch.

Do not sling your weights or swing them about. That would be very dangerous. Always move very carefully with weights (even two pound weights), and if you have never had instruction for the proper way to use them, it's crucial to do so. It is essential to incorporate all muscle groups and to balance the exercises front, back, upper, and lower body.

If you are creating your own dance with the weights, use free weights following a brief aerobic warm-up. Be sure to warm up all joints that will be used in the weight sequence for the day. Your dancing weight workout will generally take four to six songs depending on the length of the songs—approximately fifteen to twenty minutes. When you are dancing with weights, you must be able to sustain the movement, so lighter weights will be used than you might use in a traditional type of session. Many seniors (especially those who have been sedentary) will benefit greatly by using one to three pound weights. I encourage my students to go up in their weights as soon as the workout becomes easy to do. We normally do not go higher than five pound weights. Whether training traditionally or functionally, or (hopefully) both, strength training exercises should be progressive and involve all of the major muscle groups.

Find your correct posture muscles. Stand with a weight in each hand, correct all posture points—shoulders relaxed and back, belly button pushing toward the backbone, tailbone down, engaged core muscles, both front and back, neck relaxed, head in neutral, and sternum lifted. Core muscles (both front and back) are lifting up while the weights are providing resistance and pulling down.

In the medical field, it is the same as back stabilization–in other words, when your back and torso are strong and able to provide support for your entire spine and limbs—your arms and legs are going to be more fully able to move and be supported by your torso.

The American College of Sports Medicine (ACSM) and the American Heart Association (AHA) recommend strength training at least two times a week on nonconsecutive days. On a 10-point scale (0 = sitting on your couch, and 10 = carrying your couch), the level of effort should be moderate (5 to 6) to high (7 to 8). Eight to ten exercises should be performed, with a repetition range of 8 to 15 reps. The benefits of strength training with light weights are numerous. The following list will give you an idea of the importance of including weight training in your daily exercise. Sometimes seniors will say to me, "Oh, I walk every day." And, I cannot deny that walking is great exercise. However, the new science of aging suggests that it is not enough—resistance training builds strength.

And, a word to the wise—do not overlook the statement, "Strength training should be progressive." The specific overload to cause strength gains is a progressive increase in the amount of resistance used in the training program. To continue to increase strength, one must continue to increase overload. Especially for seniors who are at risk for osteoporosis, sarcopenia, or frailty, it is critical to follow the principle of progressive overload. Do not start with too much weight, and don't neglect to go up in weight when it gets too easy.

The Recognized Benefits of Weight Training

- Lowers body fat. Research in strength training has demonstrated a 4 pound fat loss after 3 months of training, even though the individuals in the study increased their daily caloric intake by 15 percent.

- Increases bone mineral density. Research has shown a significant increase in muscle, and bone and mineral content after 4 months of training.

- Improves glucose metabolism. Research has demonstrated a 23 percent improvement in glucose uptake after 4 months of strength training. The American Diabetic Association states that resistance training is critical in improving glucose clearance.

- Increases gastrointestinal transit time studies have shown a 56 percent increase in gastrointestinal transit time after 3 months of resistance training time.

- Reduces resting blood pressure. Strength training reduces resting blood pressure an average of 5 mm Hg. Both systolic and diastolic values after 2 months of training.

- Improves blood lipid levels. Several studies have revealed improved blood lipid profiles after several weeks of strength training. The improvements noted are similar for both endurance and strength exercise.

- Reduces low back pain. A 1993 study found that low back patients had significantly less back pain after 10 weeks of specific (full range) strength exercise for the lumbar spine muscles. It is important to note that over 80 percent of American adults suffer from either chronic or acute back pain.

- Reduces the pain of osteoarthritis and rheumatoid arthritis. Tufts University Diet and Nutrition Letter (1994) published a study on sensible strength training resulting in reduced pain.

- Improves balance. Recent research has proven that strength training improves the work of neurotransmitters (chemicals) in the brain that improve balance functions.

Now, it's very important for you… yes, *you,* to get started. It is time to take charge!

Resistance builds strength

Chapter Five:
The Road to Balance

Timely Tip # 5 Sitting Does Not Improve Balance

Balance is a metaphor for life: there are always going to be things that knock you off balance, but it is how you react to these knocks that determines what happens next.

As we begin the discussion about balance, it is important that we talk more about a very important part of the body—the core muscles. Good resistance training, especially with free weights, will provide core strength, but there are some other aspects that you should know.

In order to sit, stand, and walk with the minimum of difficulty, you first need to develop an accurate, conscious sense of balance. A sense of balance tells you when your body is centered. Dancers work hard to learn to center the body. Theys must have a good sense of balance in order to turn on one leg, and do many of the movements that they are required to do. We have to develop a mindset to "find center."

One normal consequence of aging is a decline in three main sensory contributors to good balance. Our sense of balance in interupted as we age by these actors:

- Vision: It is normal to have vision changes as we age.

- Proprioceptors found in tendons, muscles, ligaments and joints that provide information to the brain regarding the adjustment of posture and movement, and influence the responses required for the body to correct imbalance. Proprioception tends to change as we age.

- The tiny hairs in the semicircular canals of the inner ear that relay gravity and motion information to the brain. Hearing is often affected as we age.

Add to that the effects of many medications, and the loss of muscle strength and flexibility that typically accompany aging. The loss of balance may seem inevitable. While it is true that certain declines with age are unavoidable, physical therapists and fitness experts have repeatedly proved that much of the sense of balance can be preserved and even restored through appropriate movements and exercise. Balance is a learned skill. It is a two-fold motor skill—static while standing still, and dynamic while moving. Both are important.

You can more easily swing back into balance if you have an awareness of your center—your core—and the way you release your energy from your core. It takes practice.

When the three main bony parts of the body—the head / ribcage / pelvis—are in good alignment, they are balanced on top of one another, and the spine is in a neutral position. That means that all the curves of the spine—the cervical curve (neck), the thoracic curve (ribcage), the lumbar curve (low back), and the sacral curve (bottom of the spine)—are all in good relationship to each other and balance each other out. The cervical/ lumbar curves are in the same degree of curvature, and the thoracic / sacral curves are the same, that is, one is not more exaggerated than the other—so we are not standing in any negative postures, such as "swayback" (too much lumbar curve), or "forward head" (head jutting forward).

An important thing to remember concerning the spinal curves is that because they have to balance each other out, supporting the body's weight against gravity, if one is out of alignment, the others all have to compensate. So if you have a "forward head," too much cervical curve, the lumbar curve (it's partner, that goes in the same direction) also has to go out of alignment, and increase the extent of its curve, in order to keep the body upright.

There are many images that dance teachers often use to help students achieve this optimal alignment. I tell my youngest students, "make your body like an I, not like a C."

Older students understand, "Tail bone down, belly button towards your backbone, sternum up. Use the muscles in your glutes to support you."

You can stand sideways to a mirror and to see the effects of your body's alignment. Try this exercise. Look straight ahead and take your normal posture. Now carefully turn your head (without changing anything in your body alignment) and look at your image in the mirror. What do you see ? Most of us stand with our ribs slightly sunken back of our pelvis, and possibly in too much lumber curve ("swayback"). Imagine a line passing from the crown of the head, through the point where the skull sits on the spinal column, down through the shoulder joint, the center of gravity in the pelvis, the hip joint, the knee joint, and straight down through the heel and into the ground. Your weight on your feet should be between the big and the second tow, the little toe and the hell.

Standing evenly on both feet, make your mind a calm instrument of awareness, so that you become attentive to your bodily tensions. Notice any contortions of posture. Gently change them until you are in alignment.

Be attentive to your breathing.

Now, let yourself sway gently and slowly, backwards and forwards. Feel the whole line of your body moving softly from your ankle joints, as you sway like a tree in the wind. Feel how, if you come too far forwards you have to tense your lower back muscles in order to stay straight. If you go too far backwards, you will notice that you have to tense your stomach muscles in order to keep your balance.

Make the swaying movements smaller and smaller until you start to notice, for a fleeting moment, that you are in your optimum line of balance. Your spine feels stronger, and your head balances in a looser way on top of the spinal column. Continue to make the movements smaller and smaller until you finally come to rest in the position of perfect equilibrium.

What muscles are used when balancing? The short answer is — all of them. There are no special muscles that are used only for balancing. With balance exercises, the goal is to maintain equilibrium. The brain will activate whatever muscles it needs to help it accomplish that task. In cardio warm-ups and dancing, as you march, step touch, salsa and cha-cha, you move slightly forward, backward, and side-to-side As you move your brain is gathering information about your body's position in space. When it notices that you are leaning too far one way, it activates a group of muscles that pull you back to center.

As we learned earlier in Chapter Four, Strength training greatly improves balance. When you are weight training, chemicals in the brain, called neurotransmitters, are activated. This creates an intimate connection between your body and your brain. The neural impulses to create coordination and power create a path through your neural circuits. Each time you use them, you directly strengthen the balance, power, and muscular coordination center of the physical brain. The paths then gets broader, smoother, and faster, and that is what feels like better balance to you. Even light weights can stimulate the neurotransmitters. As you increase the amount of weight used, you then increase your strength, and that gives you more muscle power and balance for all your activities.

In both the dance and fitness world, people sometimes focus too much on the lower body–abdominals / lower back, etc.—not remembering that the upper back is equally important, and works hand in hand with the muscles we've discussed above to provide overall torso support.

Try this exercise to see how important these muscles are:

> Stand at arms length (straight arms) from a dresser, ledge, ir kitchen counter, where your hands can rest on something that is just lower than your shoulders (about chest height), palms down. Stand in your best overall alignment, with those 3 main body parts (head / ribcage / pelvis) on top of one another. Just press your hands down onto the ledge–do you immediately feel the area under your arm in back activate?

The greatest advances in balance come through movement that requires grace, agility, skill, and coordination, along with increased muscle power. To improve balance, you need controlled situations where you will be slightly unstable. During these moments of "controlled instability," your brain is learning how to coordinate the muscles of your entire body faster and more efficiently to keep you stable.

There are many ways to produce this type of instability. First, we need to think about safety. Do balance exercises in a controlled environment that stimulates your sense of balance while minimizing your risk.

During the exercises, you will put your feet in positions that may make you feel wobbly so, always stand next to something sturdy that you can hold, if necessary. Your goal is to use that support as little as possible. Hold on to your support as you position your feet and then loosen your grip and start to remove you fingers until you feel that you are challenging yourself. You can touch or tap the support while you're balancing as needed. If you need to keep a couple of fingers in contact with the support, that is fine. Always try to use it as little as possible.

Let's try a simple balance exercise. Keep one foot flat, and place just the ball of the other foot beside the heel of the flat foot. Reduce your grip and balance for 30 seconds, then do the same on the other foot. As you become more confident, raise your toe off the ground keeping your core strong and stabilizers engaged.

Now, put on some music with a catchy rhythm—the kind that makes you want to dance. Find an open space in your living room, or close to your kitchen counter. Be sure to remove any tripping hazards like magazines or shoes.

Start shifting your weight from one foot to another in time with the music. Then as you sway to your right, lift up your left foot and touch it beside your right. Then shift to the other side. Step touch, step touch. Get as fancy as you like, add some arms and shoulders into the mix. Do this for about ten minutes. Congratulations. You have just trained your balance muscles, and benefited from a ten minute cardio workout.

When I learned to dance Salsa, my instructor called it the "change your mind" step. As you begin to step out in any direction, just before you make a complete change of weight, your return to center. It is a quick little interruption in balance. For that reason, it is a good simulation of loss of balance and recovery. Balance-training programs and fall prevention interventions must include a focus on balance-recovery reactions. Ultimately it is the capability—or lack thereof—to recover from a loss of balance that eventually determines whether or not a person falls, and whether or not they can continue to live independently.

Balance disturbances can arise from collisions, slips and trips. Additionally, loss of balance can occur during voluntary movements, including bending, reaching and turning. Our body has a natural line of defense against balance disturbances called rapid limb movement. For example, reaching out to grab a supporting object or quickly stepping forward with a lower limb are compensatory mechanisms aimed at preventing a fall. Effective training programs will be those that replicate sudden balance disturbances with a quick movement back to centered control. Practice salsa dancing in all directions to practice balance recovery. Have fun!

Timely Tip #5. Sitting does not improve your balance

Chapter Six
Movement, and Your Aging Mind

Timely Tip #6 Dancing makes you smarter and healthier

This chapter may be the most important chapter in this book, though many may determine that it does not apply to themselves. Actually, it is important to each and every one of us. If doctors recognized its importance, they would write prescriptions for dancelessons, and insurance companies would pay for these lessons. The most important thing we can do for our brain is to learn to dance—any form of dance or dance fitness.

Earlier in the book, I spoke of dance in a more general way, by considering that every move we make is part of our life dance. This is a very important concept for over all wellness. The actual process of learning steps or patterns of movement is equally as important. Recent research both affirms and confirms that both the brain and the body respond positively to movement, especially dance movement. In this chapter, I will share the results of this research.

Brain cells are just like all of our cells, They go through a natural process of dying and regenerating. If we let our brains become sedentary in much the same way that we allow our bodies to become sedentary—by underuse—we lose some of that regeneration process. We, literally, lose our mind's ability to rejuvenate. There is new science of aging, newly discovered information about the brain, and we can do much to keep our brains sharp for life. Let's look at dance movement and the aging mind and body.

What I am suggesting now is that in order to gain all the benefits possible for our brain and body, we must actually learn to dance. The more intricate the choreography, the more our brain benefits. Let's look at the latest studies that provide information that can be life-changing.

Neuro-scientists are convinced that dancing is the number one activity to keep your brain sharp. Let's look at tsome of the studies that lead to that conclusion.

A 21 year study of senior citizens, 75 and older, was led by the Albert Einstein College of Medicine in New York City, funded by the National Institute on Aging, and published in the New England Journal of Medicine. Their method for objectively measuring mental acuity in aging was to monitor rates of dementia, including Alzheimer's disease, that they found.

The purpose of the study was to determine whether physical or cognitive recreational activities influenced mental acuity. They discovered that some activities had a significant beneficial effect. Other activities had none.

They studied cognitive activities such as reading books, writing for pleasure, doing crossword puzzles, playing cards, and playing musical instruments. And they studied physical activities like playing tennis or golf, swimming, bicycling, dancing, walking for exercise, and doing housework.

One of the surprises of the study was that almost none of the physical activities appeared to offer any protection against dementia. There are other health benefits, of course, but the focus of this study was the mind. There was one important exception: the only physical activity to offer protection against dementia was dancing.

Other activities studied:

Reading - 35%

Bicycling and swimming - 0%

Doing crossword puzzles at least four days a week - 47%

Playing golf - 0%

Dancing frequently - 76%

Dancing provided the greatest risk reduction of any activity studied, cognitive or physical. This study was reported in the New England Journal of Medicine in 2004.

Something about the combination of varied and demanding tasks and social engagement seem to show major benefits. Losing executive function—the ability to focus on tasks and make sound judgments—is one of the major reasons older people find themselves unable to maintain an independent lifestyle, and they are often forced to move in with family or assisted living facilities.

The key here is the emphasis on the complexity of our neuronal synapses. More is better. Do whatever you can to create new neural paths. The opposite of this is taking the same old well-worn path over and over again, with habitual patterns of thinking and living our lives. The Albert Einstein College of Medicine study shows that we need to keep as many of those paths active as we can, while also generating new paths, to maintain the complexity of our neuronal synapses.

Dr. Joseph Coyle, a Harvard Medical School psychiatrist, wrote:

> "The cerebral cortex and hippocampus, which are critical to these activities, are remarkably plastic, and they rewire themselves based upon their use." It appears that persons who dance are more resistant to the effects of dementia as a result of having greater cognitive reserve and increased complexity of neuronal synapses. The brain constantly rewires its neural pathways, as needed. If it doesn't need to, then it won't. The old expression "use it or lose it" comes to mind.

Science shows that the brain has plasticity. It can change and develop, even at advanced ages, and we are learning more about how to encourage the changes we want and discourage those we don't. Apparently, stimulating, engaging tasks challenge the brain and keep it functioning well.

Another researcher sought to determine if ballroom dance had any effect on the cognitive abilities of healthy adults. He offered ballroom dancing in an older adult community. The results of the research showed significant improvements in reasoning, visual processing, and working memory, among those involved in the classes The research concluded that dance was, indeed, a useful physical activity that also aided in mitigating stress, anxiety, and boosting social well being.

Have a look at the intelligence in dancing. The essence of intelligence may be said to be thought and making decisions. When it comes to improving your mental acuity, it is apparently important to involve yourself in activities which require thought and quick decision making, as opposed tretracing the same well-worn paths or just working on the same physical challenges over and over. Dancing integrates several brain functions at once, increasing your ability to think and act quickly. Dancing simultaneously involves,thought and decision making, an awareness of body movement, and emotional release.

How Dance Lessons Can Make You Smarter

Dancing prepares the brain for prime learning. A vigorous activity such as dancing pumps blood to the brain, giving it the glucose and oxygen it needs to function well. Apart from increasing blood flow to the brain, there is another mechanism that further improves the mental acuity of a dancer or an individual who is learning how to dance. As noted earlier, the hippocampus and the cerebral cortex—both of which play a role in dancing—are rewired and consequently improved with frequent use. The dynamism required in decision-making in dance—such as what step you need to do next—paves the way for new neural paths that make information transmission faster and better. Such activities also help improve your mental capacity since the cognitive processes are exercised in more ways than one.

What does that mean to the aging mind and body? It just means that there is much to be gained from learning like a dancer. Whether you are a beginner as far as dance goes, or you danced a great deal when you were younger, I encourage you to develop this capacity for bodily-kinesthetic learning. Take dance lessons. It is not too late.

Other Benefits of Dancing

Without a doubt, dancing can help you jumpstart your brain into overdrive. Apart from its cognitive benefits, there are other advantages that come with frequent dance lessons: Depression and stress levels are reduced. Apart from boosting your mental capacities, dancing helps you have a better outlook in life, therefore decreasing your risks of suffering from crippling stress and depression.

- Energy levels are improved because of the constant influx of the hormone serotonin. Dancing ushers a rush of the hormone serotonin, therefore giving you the energy you need to last the entire day. This is not the crash and burn feeling you get with coffee. The energy you get from dancing will surely last until sundown.

- Strength, flexibility, endurance, and balance are improved. Dancing is not only a workout for your brain, it is a great workout for your body as well. Whether you are young or old, you can enjoy improved strength, flexibility, endurance, and balance after a few sessions of dancing.

- Cardiovascular and bone health are improved. Dancing is like most physical exercises—it can improve your heart and bone health. The thing that makes it better though is that it is social and enjoyable—you can have fun with friends while enhancing your over-all health.

- Dance improves reaction time. A recent study shows that slower reaction time is associated with higher death risk in older people. We can, actually, learn how to react quickly. Using music and movement is a great way to practice. You are learning to react to some signal to your brain. It might be a count in the music, a familiar sound, or remembering choreography and repeating it to specific musical cues. When your brain will react quickly in one situation, it is apt to react quickly in another. We must be trained to move at once without needing to stop to think.

In a nutshell, dance is good for you. Researchers from Stanford University say that dancing is great at involving all the brain functions simultaneously—from musical and kinesthetic, to rational and emotional. Dancing is the perfect activity to increase neural connectivity—making you a smarter person and healthier person.

It is not enough that you dance once in awhile. An hour session at least two times a week can be benficial. With the many studies that prove the cognitive benefits of dancing, it is time to put on the music and your dancing shoes. It does not matter if you are not as graceful or as accomplished as the person standing next to you. Just remember: dancing practice makes for improved mental skills.

The bottom line is this: our bodies are meant to move. And our brains are built for novelty, and for challenges. When we challenge both our bodies and our brains, they do respond.

Dance is deeply connected with happiness. Like so many other aspects of human behavior—laughter and happiness, or handwriting and personality—dancing and happiness are closely connected. It doesn't matter what comes first. They stimulate each other. If you are happy, you feel like dancing. That's why two year old babies do those cute impromptu jigs when they are happy. Reciprocally, if you dance, you start feeling happy. Dancing lifts our mood, makes us feel positive. We are just wired that way. In my mid-sixties, I hit a bump in the road, so to speak. With some extra time on my hands, I decided to sign up for some ballroom classes. That might have been one of the best decisions of my life. All I had to do was set foot on the studio floor and I was happy, I mean really happy. What could have been a very depressing time in my life, was instead, a joyful time.

For years, as I taught Zumba®, I saw the mood of the class change as soon as I started the music. When we began dancing it was just fun. It wasn't really about learning the steps, it was about moving. It was about moving rhythmically and boldly, and about finding the patterns in the music, and matching them with movement.

Dance, while often stimulating both mind and body, can also be deeply meditative. The benefits of meditation for brain and body are well documented. Emptying the mind, temporarily disconnecting all thoughts and focusing on just the present moment is a recipe for reduced stress, better cognition, improved memory, increased creativity, and mental ability.

When you dance you are focused on the present moment,. You mY find yourself in an altered state of consciousness. For those of us who find it difficult to meditate (it is so difficult to stop your mind from wandering), dancing is a great way to find that focus without putting a lot of conscious effort into being still. When I studied for my

Master's Degree at the University of Creation Spirituality, we participated in Art As Meditation classes as part of every learning experience. Many of these classes were dance classes.

Dancing needs multiple faculties to work together. There are some important physical aspects—the lungs will be encouraged to draw in more air, the heart will be encouraged to pump blood faster, the spine and posture will become stronger, and the limbs will be encouraged to work harder. Even more importantly, the brain is challenged to work well. The ability to listen and pick the beat, get different parts of your body to continuously move and align to a rhythm is indicative of a sound, well-developed mind.

These factors may explain why dancing has been an integral part of our mating rituals too. In addition to health, dancing tells you how a person is wired. To be able to dance in co-ordination with a partner is indicative of some similarities in wiring, and compatibility. t I ran across a TV show recently called "Flirty Dancing." The show involves a participant (a young man or woman) wig us tab into the dance studio and taught dance. Then the teacher takes two people of the opposite sex from the initial participant and teaches them the same dance. Next, one couple at a time, and without saying a word, they begin to dance the movements that they learned separately. They become partners for the dance. When the dance is over, both people leave without saying a word. The same process takes place with the initial participant and the other partner. After dancing with each one of the partners, the initial participant choses one for a date. It's definitely a delightful way to get to know someone.

Dance Therapy has been used in work with traumatized patients and, patients with physical complaints like fibromyalgia and medically unexplained symptoms. It has also been used extensively in the work with elderly patients, with psychotic and schizophrenic patients, people with eating disorders, prison inmates dealing with violence and addiction issues, children and adults with different kinds of developmental disabilities, children with behavioral and relational problems, child survivors of war and torture, and also with children in regular education. Dance Therapy has also been used to reduce stress and anxiety associated with chronic diseases, like Parkinson's Disease and Cancer. Because it uses non-verbal interaction it is suggested that this treatment is especially efficient for patients whose capacity to engage in a strictly verbal therapy is limited.

My friend, Melissa Turnage, leads a program at the University of Alabama Birmingham, called Dance as Medicine. She works with individuals with a wide range of issues, both mental and physical. In the class that I take from her at a home for the older adult and handicapped persons, she inclusively incorporates students in wheelchairs, power chairs, walkers, canes, the deaf, in addition to fully functioning people. Performances by this unique group are always a big hit. Dance is a universal language.

We know that dancing makes us happy, makes us feel good. Being in a happy state is good for our overall health.

Will you move? Are you ready to dance with the fire burning in you? If you want to transform your life, you will choose to move. You can not change when you are rigid. Let that inner fire change your stiffness into a dance.

Now you know that you were born a dancer. You are capable of bending, stretching, letting go, circling and kicking. Long before you could talk or walk you were dancing. Relax now, anticipate and enjoy the rhythm. Listen carefully and you can hear your heart beat. Call it your dance of life.

Perhaps it sounds like I am speaking metaphorically. This is partially true, but actual dancing will move you forward. As I mentioned earlier, when I was sixty-seven years old, I stopped teaching ballet for a while. My life made an abrupt halt. Everything I knew about who I was stopped. Life seemed empty and I felt empty. At first I floundered around and looked back at the past trying to discover what went wrong, and just who I was without teaching dance, and then I decided to discover who I was by dancing. I called the closest Fred Astaire Studio and signed up for some classes. It was there I met Michael Hosale, a young instructor who would become my teacher. Though I had taught ballroom dancing when I was in college, it had been so many years ago that everything had changed. Oh, a Cha Cha beat was still a Cha Cha beat, but the moves had changed and I found myself a beginner. My first lessons included Cha Cha, Fox Trot and a little East Coast Swing, but my favorite was the Cha Cha. Michael encouraged me to move boldly (well, actually, he meant to move with a sexy freedom, but to me, a prude at 67, that meant boldly).

That next six months was nothing short of a total transformation for me. I was moving boldly and I was not looking back. I discovered that I was still a dancer at the very soul of me, and that I could use that to move forward in my life. In fact, one of the things Michael reminded me each time we started to dance, "Poise forward." When he asked me why I liked to dance, I answered, "It releases my soul!"

In addition to the benefits for the brain, and the body let's look beneath these benefit to the deeper benefits that have been recently discovered as described by Dr. Mark Liponis, author of *UltraLongevity: The Seven-step Program for a Younger, Healthier You*. Dance is Step Number 4... right next to Breathing and Eating.

Rhythmic movement or moving to a particular rhythm is the essence of any dance. The most important new discoveries about movement confirm that it offers benefits across a wide range of health conditions, and has a positive impact on the immune system and on aging itself. Dancing, rather than just moving, has been shown to have the greatest effect on CRP levels (in other words it reduces inflammation). Further studies show that adding music to the rehabilitation of Parkinson's Disease patients has improved outcome when compared with standard physical therapy. Participants receiving music/dance therapy also scored higher on a happiness measure. When we are breathing well, we are breathing rhythmically. Or, consider the body's most obvious rhythm: the heartbeat. Loss of normal heart rhythm has also been linked with immune activation. Dance improves everything from our balance and gait to bone density in the legs and hips. It creates a better mood. It's been shown to help with weight loss and to improve cardiovascular fitness. It lowers cholesterol levels and, it reduces pain. Dance movement may well be the closest thing to the Fountain of Youth ever studied. (Dr. Mark Liponis)

It is clear that dance offers many benefits for older adults. Remember it doesn't matter what kind of dance or, how well you dance. Let dancing become a consistent part of your life.

Dancing makes you smarter and healthier

Chapter Seven
Your Spirit Burns Within

Timely Tip #7 This Could be Your Best Season

Luscious fruit in summer, the moon in autumn, the sparkling snow in winter, a thousand flowers in spring… this could be the best season of your life.

-- inspired by Japanese poetry

The seasons naturally draw us into honoring creation and our Creator. Just think of the continuous creativity of the still evolving, unfolding, universe story. Embrace your relationship with nature and the Earth, to live and work soulfully. Infuse each day with creativity, living as if creativity matters—indeed, as if creation matters. Our creativity binds with creation uniting us with the Divine, telling our personal creation stories. Your spirit burns within you and longs to tell your story.

The stories we carry within give witness to understanding the universe as sacred. When we embody these stories in poetry, d art, drama, and dance, they become reflections that draw us deeper into ourselves and closer to the Creator. This kind of creative energy is playful and pleasure filled. When we become deeply engaged in creative activity, we enjoy knowing the presence of God.

I had the pleasure during the pandemic of 2020, to watch just such a creative process. My daughter, Cindy Free, was the Director of the Birmingham Ballet Academy. Each year the school ends its season with a Showcase in the form of a story ballet featuring its students. This year's story was

Alice in Wonderland, a story where a child's dream takes her to a wacky land where nothing is normal. We (I am an instructor on the staff of BBA) were in the process of teaching dances to our young students. Costumes had been ordered and most had come in, or were on the way. Then suddenly we were told we must shelter in place because of the pandemic. No more classes in the studio. We quickly switched to a Zoom format and continued to work on our Showcase pieces not knowing how, or if, the event would ever take place. Cindy was eager to make it happen, and decided that the answer was film and the out-of-doors. She chose beautiful Aldridge Gardens in Hoover, AL as her stage and set. In small groups over a period of two weeks, every individual class came to the park and, without any further rehearsal, danced their roles in the garden. I watched in awe as the pieces came together finalizing in a video for all to see. God's creation and Cindy's creativity combined to give birth to story. Yes, the story involved a time in a wacky land, where nothing is normal—perhaps, a time when everyone is sheltered at home because of pandemic. And yet, in the very midst of it, God's creative presence was evident, The production of Alice in Wonderland ushered in Summer and suddenly became one of its "luscious" fruits. I asked Cindy if this was a "spiritual" event for her, and her answer was, "Oh my yes. Every step of the way."

Without a flame that is spirit burning brightly within us, we will soon give in to our frail earthly selves. We are not an earthly body with a heavenly spirit; we are a heavenly spirit with an earthly body. Look at the importance of nurturing spirit. How does the short Japanese poem above speak to you and your spirit? Are you in the best season of your life? Let's start right out by discovering the answer to that question.

Medical science reports that people who meditate or pray contemplatively have lower blood pressure than those who do not. Perhaps that's because meditation encompasses body, mind and spirit. There are many different forms of meditation. We will explore just two of them—simple reflection, and reflection combined with story and movement. Simple reflection requires nothing but a quiet place.

Read the poem again.

Luscious fruit in summer,

the moon in autumn,

the sparkling snow in winter,

a thousand flowers in spring…

this could be the best season of your life.

Could this be the best season of your life?

The First Meditations/Reflections

Find a quiet place for yourself where you can take each phrase of this poem and reflect or meditate on it. Take your time. Reflect on no more than one phrase each day. One phrase may speak to you more than another. Regardless of the weather outside, that season that speaks to you may be your present season. Enjoy its beauty! The inevitable changes of the seasons speak to us. In wordless messages they speak to those who listen with their hearts. The messages are not vague and difficult to interpret. They require only that we stop long enough to notice them. Start by reflecting on each phrase. Reflecting means to look back. Look back into your own life experience, your story, and ponder the meaning of each phrase.

From your reflections, I will suppose that you have determined which season of the year is the season that most speaks to you, and about you, at this time. If you have not determined which season is yours at the moment, choose one to explore in a new way now. In fact, it might be interesting to do each one and see which one speaks to you the most.

Story and Dance

As we enter this section, try to let go of any preconceived concepts of what meditation is, and what dance is. Any form of creativity drawing us closer to God is a meditation, especially if it brings us to know God and ourselves in a deeper way. Allow yourself to move without judgement. Move with your own natural movement language. You might even find a child (or the child within you) to join the dance. Children know the language of movement. So do you if you let yourself rediscover the joy. There is no right or wrong way to do this. Literally, dance as though no one is watching. Let that flame that changes stiffness into a dance burn within you. On a personal note, when I first started doing this in my basement as a teenager, I felt that it was perhaps, heretical. It is not. God loves our dances. You can dance with or without music. You might dance in silence and add music later. There is no one way. You are dancing for the process, not the product. Let it become a process that continues to burn within you and push you out of any stiffness you might feel. Use the Meditation Stretch in the Appendix to get your body and mind ready to move. You may want to use the ideas in the Appendix under Elements of Dance to help you create your dance.

Luscious Fruit in Summer... In Summer we are aware of abundance. It is a place of fulfillment and of deep contemplation. Nature is able to accomplish a great deal in a small amount of time in the summer. Summer is a time of profuse growth and at the same time, as the shadows deepen, we also see color and life and energy. When the shadows deepen we can look more closely at them, perhaps finding the courage to speak to them. "The beliefs and ghosts of the past haunt the present as it stretches into the future. The eerie, shifting image of Shadow appears where there is light and fire and a storyteller to bring it to life." Both enchanted and frightened by our shadows, our past darkness affects our present life. Unless we face our shadows, speak to them, and make story of them, we carry them into our future. When you choose to enter the second phase of our meditations, Meditation with Story and Dance, you may want to create a Shadow dance that takes you out of the past and into the future. It may take you outside where you can see your shadow and other shadows. Allow your own story of abundance or shadow to emerge.

The first time I did this meditation, I clearly found myself in the summer season. Summer holds my spiritual roots; it is the season when I am most happy. It is a place of fulfillment, and both a time of pleasure and of deep contemplation. As I read the poem, I decided to visualize a favorite place in nature where I could feel totally relaxed and at peace. I wanted to go to the beach, a place I love, but that was not where my soul wanted to go. I wrote these words in my journal following the experience: "I was immediately taken to the waterfall rocks at Camp Winnataska, though I tried to go to the beach. The images were very clear. I am a child drinking spicy tea from a tin cup. From this rock I can see the bridge, the waterfall, and Hillside where Vesper services are held. The rock warms my bare feet." This is a special place, the birthplace of my spiritual journey, as I know it. I walked barefoot those days at camp feeling the cool earth beneath my feet, stubbing my toes on tree roots, and feeling the warmth of the shallow water as I sat on the rocks by the waterfall. Camp images linger even now. Images from a song we sang at Winnataska—"When it's darkness at Winnataska, that's the time my heart is full, when it's darkness at Winnataska, let me linger there beside the waterfall… " Yes, let me linger in summer knowing that autumn will soon come with its challenges, its transitions and changes. Who knows what deep secrets the next winter holds, and then the full rich promises of spring? But summer —this may be the best season. I will dance the feeling of the "laughing waters" of the waterfall.

A Thousand flowers in spring…For many people, it is the blossoming flowers that truly announce the arrival of spring. Most of us hurry to finish whatever it is that our busy lives require so that we can get outside and enjoy the early warmth of the sun. Something happens to our hearts on a warm Spring day. Suddenly we have new energy for the dance of life. In Spring, we are aware of our growth, we are aware that little by little changes are happening within us, we are aware of beauty all around us. In spring, it is easy to be grateful for life. You may wish to just give time to reflecting on the many things for which you are grateful. If you find that feel most like you are in Spring, you might create a dance using the verbs and descriptions in this poem by Mary Oliver to create your dance.

The Sunflowers

Come with me into the field of sunflowers.

Their faces are burnished disks, Their dry spines

creak like ship masts, their green leaves,

so heavy and many, fill all day with the sticky

sugars of the sun.

Come with me to visit the sunflowers,

they are shy but want to be friends;

they have stories of when they were young-

the important weather, the wandering crows.

Don't be afraid to ask them questions!

Their bright faces, which follow the sun,

will listen and all those rows of seeds..

each one a new life! hope for a deeper acquaintance,

each of them, though it stands in a crowd of many,

like a separate universe ,is lonely, the long work

of turning their lives into a celebration, It is not easy.

Come and let us talk with those modest faces,

the simple garment of leaves, the coarse roots in the earth

so uprightly burning.

The moon in autumn... No artist can truly duplicate the spectacular scene we witness as autumn arrives in all its brilliance. In many parts of our country we are showered with the beauty of the Earth's colors. The brilliant red, yellow and orange leaves mingle and merge with the deep brown or red of the Earth itself with the richness of the evergreens creating a scene quite beyond our imaginations—a true gift of the Universe. Like the leaves and the phases of the moon, we are called to transformation.

Prayer for Autumn Days

God of the seasons, there is a time for everything; there is a time for dying and a time for rising. We need courage to enter into the transformation process.

God of autumn, the trees are saying goodbye to their green, letting go of what has been. We, too, have our moments of surrender, with all their insecurity and risk. Help us to let go when we need to do so.

God of fallen leaves lying in colored patterns on the ground, our lives have their own patterns. As we see the patterns of our own growth, may we learn from them.

God of misty days and harvest moon nights, there is always the dimension of mystery and wonder in our lives. We always need to recognize your power-filled presence. May we gain strength from this.

God of harvest wagons and fields of ripened grain, many gifts of growth lie within the season of our surrender. We must wait for harvest in faith and hope. Grant us patience when we do not see the blessings.

God of geese going south for another season, your wisdom enables us to know what needs to be left behind and what needs to be carried into the future. We yearn for insight and vision.

God of flowers touched with frost and windows wearing white designs, may your love keep our hearts from growing cold in the empty seasons.

God of life, you believe in us, you enrich us, you entrust us with the freedom to choose life. For all this, we are grateful.

And, when you are ready to move into Autumn, dance this prayer thinking of your own transformation. You might want to use gentle, flowing music (preferably instrumental) like "The Autumn Leaves."

The Sparkling snow in winter... Winter calls us to attempt to understand living. What responsibilities does living evoke? How do we live creating light in a time of darkness?

Throughout history, and across many cultures, the Winter Solstice remains one of the most important festivals of the year. It is the time to honor the sun and encourage its return after the darkness of winter. It was once believed human beings need to contribute their energy in order to coax the sun back—not really a bad idea. If we are fortunate enough to have the opportunity to enjoy at least a day or two of snow in this season, we need only to look at the amazing differences in the individual snowflakes that make up the blanket of snow, and we cannot help but appreciate diversity. In winter we experience many opportunities at life with a new perspective—to see diversity instead of sameness, to feel the warmth of compassion instead of cold insensitivity; to do justice instead of sitting in judgement; to create light instead of fearing darkness.

Create a dance of light. Try to show your understanding of the concept of coaxing the sun back after darks days. Show that you understand diversity and that new perspective sheds light and leads to compassion and justice.

Falling in love with the natural changes of the seasons of life will renew and refresh our love of life itself.

Combining story, dance, and meditation introduces a style of reflection that involves both movement and stillness. In the previous section, I have given suggestions that you might use for moving into this type of meditation. For those searching for a deep relationship with God, the process involves using poetry, prayer, and story to journey toward a close communion with the Creator by using simple movement patterns that you can create for yourself. The process may at first, take you out of your comfort zone, but that is not a bad thing. No one is judging you. Go back to the poem, reflect and then move.

Steps to Spiritual Wellness and Wholeness

- Explore your spiritual core—Ask yourself the big questions: Who am I? Why did I come here? Why do humans/the world exist? Why is there evil? What happens after death? Your answers to these questions will reveal your spiritual core.

- Be quiet—Spend time alone and meditate regularly. Meditation is the process of being fully here, with all concentration focused on the now. By living in the present and letting go of the past and not worrying about the future, we can achieve the inner peace that we strive for w h i l e practicing meditation. If stillness is difficult for you, try a movement meditation.

- Be inquisitive and curious—an attitude of active searching increases your options and your potential for spiritual centering. Don't shut doors before you check out what's behind them.

- Be receptive to grief and pain—Pain is deepening.. Allow yourself to feel the pain fully, then ask what it's trying to teach you.

- Witness the choices you make in each moment—Bring them into consciousness; ask yourself what the consequences of a choice are and if the choice will bring fulfillment and happiness. Listen with your heart and be guided by messages of comfort and discomfort. If there is comfort, go for it. If there is discomfort, pause and reevaluate.

- Practice acceptance—See that life right now is as it "should be." Do not struggle against the universe by struggling against the moment. Take responsibility for your life without blaming anyone, including yourself. See what the situation can teach you and how you can share this teaching with others.

- Practice detachment—Allow yourself and those around you the freedom to be who they are. Recognize uncertainty as an essential aspect of life. See that solutions come out of problems, confusion, and chaos, and that uncertainty is the path to freedom.

- Be playful—Spirituality is in music, art, dance, laughter, singing, and all of life.

- Look for deeper meanings—If you notice that certain themes keep coming up over and over in your life, rather than feeling like you have no control over the situation, ask for the deeper meaning of the pattern to come to you. See the gift in your greatest troubles/problems/challenges. The Chinese word for catastrophe is the same as their word for opportunity.

- Take "seven breath" breaks—Stop periodically throughout the day, close your eyes, and take seven deep breaths (breathe in slowly through your nose for seven counts, let the air out through your mouth for seven counts; do seven slow breaths this way). Then open your eyes and see your new world.

Find your story within the seasons. Circle back to the beginning of this chapter and see which season holds your attention the most. Explore that season with your own creativity, your own story. God works through us awakening the soul, rhythming the heart, and allowing for the changing and growing self. Pay attention!* As a footnote to this chapter—today, I find myself in Winter. I find myself being called to attempt to understand living. What responsibilities does living evoke? How can I live creating light in a time of darkness? This pandemic and the cultural struggles that identify this time in history are times of deep darkness. Aging, especially when one's eyes are failing, brings on thoughts of darkness. Perhaps my dance can coax the sun back—bring myself and others into the light. I wonder, what's net?

This could be your best season

Chapter Eight
Where Does Your Heart Lie?

Timely Tip #8 *Come now and listen to your heart*

There is a strong parallel between the dynamic creativity known as passion that keeps our spirits alive, and the pumping heart that keeps our bodies alive.

The heart is a strong, muscular pump a little larger than a fist. It is only one part of the larger circulatory system that includes the lungs, arteries, arterioles (small arteries), capillaries, venules (small veins), and veins. The heart is continually working to move blood throughout the circulatory system including the arteries that feed the heart. In fact, it beats over 100,000 times and pumps over 2,000 gallons of blood each day.

Physical death comes quickly if the pumping described above stops. Likewise, spiritual death is near if the lifeblood, the creativity, the passion that nourishes our spirits stops circulating. We are spirits with bodies, not bodies with spirits. We must be at least as concerned with the health of our creative passionate heart as we are with the well being of the muscular pump that sustains our lives. Life is a song, a dance, or a poem, waiting to be sung, danced, or written. It is a loom with the warp in place, waiting for color, life, and energy. It is a pot, a picture, a garden, waiting to be thrown, painted, planted. Where does your heart lie?

When we create, the energy of our work is connected to the moment of Creation. Creation opens the door to our creativity. God goes to the same place to create the planet on which we live, a galaxy of stars, or a human baby, as He goes to create a thought or image in our minds. The cosmos unveils the most exciting parable, the call to creativity. It speaks to us like an artist's rendering, "Come now and listen to your heart." Matthew Fox explains: "To be in touch with our hearts is to be in touch with the heart of the universe and the heart of the Divine Creator." When we create, we find ourselves close to God.

Living soulfully means infusing each day with creativity, living as if creativity matters—as if Creation matters. Children know instinctively that Creation matters and they are incessantly creative. It is the way they find out who they are, and what they can do. When and how do we stop valuing our innate creativity, our innate passions? It often happens when we are quite young, in schools, in daycares, in churches and worse, in our own families. The natural connections weaving together cosmos, spirit, and self are destroyed by indifference, and sometimes, even ridicule. Once torn, they are difficult to repair unless, at some deep level, we remember and reclaim the connections.

I thought I knew my grandson well. I had been with him on a regular basis since he was born. I learned that there was much I didn't understand, and even his immediate family was surprised when he said to us one evening at dinner, "It's cars! You have to understand, I really dig cars, and I want to get a car that I can race in Autocross races." This seemed like a sudden passion for cars. After all, he was an accomplished pianist, a dancer, too. Wasn't he most interested in the arts? He assured us that his passion for cars had been there since very early on. We just did not notice. He was a Junior in High School when he courageously acknowledged and insisted on his passion. It came after he was asked what he would choose as his major in college.

He tells this story of his decision. "I went into my bedroom and looking around I asked myself 'what is important to me?'" He looked at the shelves of Lego cars and airplanes that he had built. He looked at the paintings of race cars on his walls, he looked at his ceiling painting with stars, and remembered his love of the night sky. He pondered and decided this: "I want to build and design things that go fast… perhaps even rockets to take me into space." He ended up at Georgia Tech with a major in Mechanical Engineering and a minor in Aerospace Engineering. Now, he has adjusted his initial dreams as he discovered his innate love for the planet. Now, as his master's project, he is designing cars that still go fast, and are also environmentally friendly. These connections in his life were and are primal connections. They are part of who he is at his very core. While at Georgia Tech, he was part of a group that built a race car and raced in an international competition. Racing is definitely an important part of his life.

While Kit had to purposely discover and reveal his passion, Katherine, my granddaughter, revealed her passions at an early age (at least one of them). She speaks of doing a "face-plant" while trying to dance like the advanced dancers, even before she could walk. I have always told Kat that she dances from the inside out. Her heart and soul is always revealed in her dancing. As a young dancer she had many opportunities to travel. Her visits to other countries developed a passion for other cultures. In addition to being a dance professional, she she studied Global Business Relations. Now, she works in Global Business, and still dances. Just this

As I mentioned earlier in this book, as a very young child, I wanted to dance. In my teens, I began to teach ballet and tap dancing. The innate teacher part of me was ready. I loved sharing my passion for dance with children. I still do. I taught dance until I was eighty-six years of age. It looks like that part of me may have to be adjusted in the coming years though it will always be a part of me. I wonder what new form it may take. As my body weakens and my eyes dim, how will I reclaim that passion? An answer to that question is yet to come, and I look forward to discovering and shaping it.

Reclaim your innate passions as you age. If long ago you gave them up, listen to your heart and find them again. Open the eyes of your heart, and see them again.

Our emotions are heart-centered.

Long ago, my good friend, John Begg, choreographed a ballet call *Pierrot et son Coeur* — translated, "Pierrot and His Heart," Four lovely girls in pink tutus snatched Pierrot's heart away from him and began to toss it around and play with it. Of course, they ended up breaking poor Pierrot's heart. What emotions play with your heart? What breaks your heart? What heals your heart?

When I was a teenager, Mom said, "You think too much!" Daddy said, "You wear your heart on your sleeve." Mixed messages for me, but they were probably both right. Every teenager appears to think too much and to be too emotional. I saw it in my own children and grandchildren at that age. It is part of growth, an important part of getting to know oneself. Am I still getting to know myself? The answer is, "yes." If we truly set out to take charge of our lives, we will continue to grow and to learn new things about ourselves.

At no time in my life though, do I remember wearing my heart on my sleeve in the way that I do in my eighties. Life is precarious and everything is uncertain. If I don't take charge of dealing with these emotions, they could be my demise. Here are some of the emotions that sometimes overwhelm me — perhaps a few may ring true with you, or you may have your own list. Mine are fear, loneliness, anxiety, frustration, and stress.

In my eighties, it's like living the terrible twos and the early teens all over again, with all the uncontrolled emotion that earmarks those stagesof life.

Let go of your fears, resentments, regrets, and sadness to find your heart's beauty. Yes, that's a tall order.

Keep life on the light side by living more in the present, in the moment. Tackle the task of living easily with uncertainty. In fact, rejoice in the freedom of uncertainty. In the days of the pandemic, I found this concept of the "freedom of uncertainty" compelling. Never has life been so uncertain.

Intentional living with passion, compassion and creativity releases emotions in positive ways.

What is Compassion?

Heather Winkle, Vice President of Design, Capital One, describes compassion in this way.

> *"So remember that compassion is a "fellow feeling," whether that fellow is a customer, a teammate, or yourself. Compassion channels your creative energy*

not just toward solutions, but toward discovering the real problem by observing and understanding. Compassion enables you to create a beacon to not just align but connect your team to a shared solution. ***Compassion is a reminder to dive deeper than the surface solution and tap into a place of authentic caring.*** *You'll be amazed at how things start to line up and everything feels easier and has real purpose. Most importantly, you can tap into and harness your creative energy in a way that is sustainable, satisfying, and exciting. And from that place of creative compassion, you will bring some pretty incredible ideas into the world."*

Compassion and creativity go hand in hand. When you play music, and begin to dance to it, something happens that takes away insanity and it becomes "fellow feeling"—compassion! I remember the surge of emotion that I felt at a Zumba® convention when thousands of people danced together. We were one feeling—one heart, full of passion. That is the feeling of compassion, when your heart overflows with others.

When I described myself earlier, as a dancer, a writer, a teacher, and a storyteller, I realize those things haven't changed. They have moved in different directions, taken different shapes, and taken different forms, but in my heart I have always been a dancer, a writer, a teacher and a storyteller. I literally, love these parts of me. They are my passions. When I use these passions for others, or with others, they become acts of compassion.

Sometimes our passions take us beyond the expectations of others, our own expectations, and even, beyond our wildest dreams. A few years ago, I watched as Tara Lipinski, 15-year-old figure skater, rose beyond all expectations and captured an Olympic gold medal. It was a rather mystical 4 1/2 minutes. Tara seemed to be at one with her passion. It appeared to me that her skating, in that brief time, no longer had anything to do with an act of her will. Yes, she had trained hard, and in the training process there was much will and skill involved. But at that moment in time, I watched her stand out of her own way, letting her passion carry her, taking her to a place beyond all expectations, a mystical place where the results were out of her hands. When it was over she said, " Well, that was cool," as if she had nothing to do with it. There was even an apparent humility that looked at what she had done and stood in awe of it.

Standing out of one's own way is important. I am at my worst when I am trying to live up to the expectations of others, and even trying to live up to my expectations of myself. If I can stand out of my way, and let my creativity and passion take over, the results are much better. Do you find yourself getting in your own way sometimes? Stand back. Let your passion soar. Aging well calls for courage. Growing young into old age, is an achievement, a work of art, that requires your passion and creativity. I read a meme on Facebook today. "You can be a Masterpiece and a Work in Progress at the same time." My immediate response was "thank goodness." That's exactly where we are. As we age, we've been around long enough to be a Masterpiece, but if we are aging well, we are courageous enough to be a Work in Progress. Look for your heart's language.

The Language of the Heart

The heart expresses itself through creativity. I have mentioned dance and for me, that is where my heart expresses itself. Others find creativity in an infinite number of passions. There is no right or wrong way to be creative. What are you doing when your heart overflows?

The Village of the Arts and Humanities was founded by Lily Yeh, an artist and Chinese immigrant who was a tenured professor at the Philadelphia School of Fine Arts. The village has renovated dozens of urban lots and empty buildings with murals, mosaics, and gardens. *"When people see beauty, they cherish it. The heart of the Village is art. Art is creativity–in thinking, planning, strategizing, and implementation. We want to create a new urban village of beauty, where people have meaningful jobs, live in decent houses, grow their own food, and raise the next generation of greeners."* It is clear that in this community, creativity is a driving force that keeps the village alive. *"On the rough palette of North Philadelphia, the once vacant lots touched by the magic of the* **Village of Arts and Humanities** *sparkle like stars on a crisp winter night. With a phantasmagoria of mosaic sculptures, murals and gardens glimmering with giant angels and creatures no zoo has ever seen, the Village offers vibrant testimony to the role that art can play in bringing a desolate urban landscape back to life and engaging youth and families in the arts."*

While pursuing my Master's Degree, I had the opportunity to study with Lily Yeh. She spoke of how she came to this neighborhood in 1986 to paint a mural of Creation on the barren outside wall of a dance studio run by Arthur Hall, a choreographer and impresario who earned fame bringing African dance to American stages. Their passions met and collaborated and soon a whole village was involved. This is the beauty of creativity and compassion. When the two meet, the language of the heart is speaking. When Lily spoke, it was easy to feel her heart overflowing. She later gave up her tenured position to tend the gardens in the Village. The village still exists today with thrivip rograms supporting the arts with a mission to imagine, design and build a more just and ethical society.

Reflections on Creation

It seems important as we look at creativity and compassion to reflect for a moment on Creation. For years, if someone asked me to reflect on something, I just thought it meant to think about that thing. But, the word reflect carries deeper meaning. Something that reflects comes back to you. If you look in a mirror, you will see your reflected image. If you reflect on your past experiences, you look at them once again, thoughtfully. If we reflect on Creation, we look again and see anew.

Let's take some time to consider our own role in the unfolding story of Creation. It is constantly evolving and we are called to do the same. Listen and reflect on the song, the dance, the poem you are longing to sing, dance or write. Your life is a canvas ready for color and energy. Set aside some time each day to rejoice in your Creator, and in your own creativity.

Author, Clarissa Pinkola Estes writes, *"I've seen women who insist on cleaning everything in the house before they could sit down to write. And you know it is a funny thing about housecleaning, it never comes to an end. Perfect way to stop a woman. A woman must be careful to not allow over-responsibility (or over-respectability) to steal her necessary creative rests, riffs, and raptures. She simply must put her foot down and say "no" to half of what she believes she should be doing. Art is not meant to be created for stolen moments only."*

God tells us how he felt when he created the world. Over and over he rejoices in all that he has made. He made us in His image, and we are called to co-create the world joyfully. He has placed it on our hearts to be co-creators. And, to celebrate with Him saying "That is good!"

What do we know about Creation? Let's begin at the beginning. We'll start with ancient times. Cultural touchstones such as creation stories are important ways in which traditional knowledge is shared. A creation myth or story is a cultural, traditional, or religious, myth that describes the earliest beginnings of the present world. Myths like these are usually developed first in the oral tradition, and are found throughout human culture.

Creation stories are a way of trying to explain our beginnings, and the way things are. Many creation stories have a great deal of violence in them. Some are humorous. Creation stories were incredibly important in the ancient world (and now), because they rooted and grounded you in a particular view of who you are and what you are doing here. They express our innate knowings.

Let's think now about the first chapter of Genesis that we know as our biblical Creation Story. It was edited together when the Israelites found themselves in exile in Babylon.

The Babylonians had a creation story called the Enuma Elish. In the Enuma Elish, the god Marduk defeated the goddess Tiamt and then tore her carcass apart, using the two halves to make the world. Pretty violent. At the heart of the

Babylonian story was an understanding that violence is the engine of creation. That's how the world was created—that's how we got here.

Now, the Israelites were conquered by those Babylonians and hauled away from their homeland to the foreign world of Babylon where they were trying to maintain their sense of identity and tribe, while surrounded by the dominant culture and the stories of Babylon.

And what do they do in exile? They begin to compile the Hebrew scriptures which begin with their tribe's creation story. This scripture in Genesis, the biblical Creation Story is a poem. It is a poem in which beauty, diversity, difference, and order, are celebrated. A poem in which the engine of creation is Divine Joy—not destruction, but overflowing generosity—not with violence, but with joy.

Think of the beautiful picture of God taking the dust from the ground, shaping it into his own image and breathing into the breath of life. We are all breathed into life by the Divine. To find our creation stories, we create. What is important to you? How can you bring that to the world? Combine your deepest soul longings with those of others, and you are not only creative, but compassionate. Together, our creativity and our compassion shape a better world.

I had the joy of engaging in such a collaboration. A few years ago, I invited some of my senior fitness students to take part in an experiment with me. For six weeks we would be involved in a creative dance project. I called it Ageless Adventures in Movement. For the most part, the women who came would call themselves non-dancers. We came together to explore aging though creating dances about aging. After about three weeks, I told the "dancers" that since dance is a performing art we would perform our "explorations" for the senior center. That was a surprise to everyone, but they agreed, and we were able to share our creative process with others. It felt good. And we continued that process for three years visiting many senior centers and retirement homes to share the things we were learning about aging. Our hearts met the hearts of those for whom we danced. We discovered new purpose. We danced a piece of choreography in which we changed from cocoons into butterflies. The piece was called "Your Time as a Cocoon is Over." Aging is a time to take wings and "fly."

Listen to the pulsing of your heart. It is spirit and passion. It's pulse and energy. Pay attention to it. Notice whether you are just plodding along through life, or moving with a dynamic energy. Strangely enough, the more energy you use, the more you get. Your creativity produces new energy.

Come now and listen to your heart

Chapter Nine

All CreationAwaitsYou

Timely Tip #9 Value Your Connections

Many indigenous groups use the phrase "all my relations" that reflects people who are aware that everything in the universe is connected. Your love (or simply connection) can lead to important relationships, and it may lead you to uncommon service. How do you connect to the world around you? How do you love the world, those around you, and your self? All creation awaits your presence. All creation awaits your connection, your love.

The most important connection we make is our connection to our Creator. Next in importance to us are the relationships we enjoy with family and friends,N.ext is the diverse community in which we live and function As we age, we often lose contact with many of these connections that were once important. It is valuable for us to stay connected. It is key to healthy aging—value your connections. Studies have shown that older people who have close connections and relationships not only live longer, but also cope better with health conditions, and experience less depression. Life transitions can impact the number and quality of people's social and community networks. A life that maximizes social interaction and human-to-human contact is good for the brain at every stage, particularly for the aging brain. We now know that people who have more social support tend to have better mental health, cardiovascular health, immunological functioning, and cognitive performance. Let's look at some of the networks we have created over the years, and some that might be important to create.

Social activities act as a cognitive stimulus as we age. We value these activities that keep us mentally sharp. As our social relationships shrink over time because of retirement, divorce, illness, and death, it is important that we have diverse ties that keep us from losing connection. Social ties provide a way or the exchange of emotional, psychological, and material support. Social support offers a sense of belonging that allows us to cope well with stressful situations.

These days we have the possibility of enjoying virtual social connection through social media friendships, and through meetings on Zoom and other meeting formats. I have three high school friends that I meet with each moth on Zoom.Though it is often frustrating because of our varying technical skills, it is still rewarding to keep up with these friends who now live thousands of miles apart. Our seventieth high school reunion is next year (2024).

Every day I enjoy the connections that I make on Facebook. I value that Facebook friends help me to feel connected. I can connect with people from all over the world, and people that I have not seen in years, but still enjoy their relationship. I connect with former students, former classmates, and former Zumba® buddies. I have been stimulated by the conversations with many of these "friends." Do not overlook these virtual opportunities. They may be just the thing to keep you from being lonely. Even the very act of learning how to keep up with technology can be a socially engaging activity.

During the pandemic of 2020, it we depended on these virtual connections since we were under stay at home or safer at home orders. Our connections with those we love were stifled, at best. We could hug those we love, we could not shake hands in greeting. We wore masks and we could not even see the smiles of the people we had the rare chance to see. Perhaps it is a good time to look at the fact that we are connected to all God's creation.

Connections to the Creator

Sometimes the pieces of our story take a long time to connect to one another. Like fitting together a puzzle, the picture may take a long time to complete. Let me tell you a part of my story of finding a church by connecting to God. When I was a child, my family didn't attend church often. When I was six years old, I attended Camp Winnataska summer camp in Alabama. This was a camp organized, at that time, by The Birmingham Sunday School Council, an ecumenical group. It was there that I realized that I was a Christian, that I had a deep faith that was nurtured there through Native American tales, stories of Knights of the Round Table in search of the Holy Grail, and by Bible Study, Vesper Services, and on Sunday,

Worship at the Cross. What happened at camp that summer began to shape me. At home, after camp, I found that many of my young friends went to church with their families and I would beg to go with them. Every summer I went back to Winnataska, and my faith continued to grow. My search for "my" church began even then. My mother came from a Methodist family, my father from a Presbyterian family, (I heard that Granddaddy had been a choir boy in the Scottish Presbyterian Church in Saltcoates, Scotland), so that meant that we were Protestants. Over the years as I grew and searched, I attended and even joined, many different churches.

I became a Methodist, a Presbyterian, an Episcopalian, a Methodist again, Assembly of God member, and again, a Methodist. For 21 years I attended my son's church, a Southern Baptist Church, but through all of these experiences, my spirit never felt totally at home. Then, just a few years ago, I visited a Christian Church (Disciples of Christ), and found my soul rejoicing. I am finally in what I feel in my heart and soul is my home church. To my surprise, I discovered this denomination has its roots in the Scottish Presbyterian Church, my grandfather's church. Is that a coincidence? Well, possibly. Yet, I do think there may be more to it than that. Now I look forward to the rest of this story! How will I grow and serve in my church home"

Connections to Nature

In his book, Ultralongevity, Dr. Mark Liponis says that a connection to nature is very important to your health.

"Love can mean love of nature. It can mean a feeling of oneness with the world. It can denote that warm, fuzzy emotion you have when doing something as simple as appreciating a cozy fireplace on a cold morning." We may need to broaden what we value as connections.

Can we value nature as a connection? Lately, when I am talking to my daughter on the phone, she interjects information about what the birds and chipmunks are doing in her yard. They have, literally, become her friends. I get the daily report on them as often as I get the report on my grandchildren. The Earth has been a source of connection since the moment of Creation. Perhaps we are being called to notice. Have you ever noticed a sense of well-being both emotionally and physically, while, or after taking a walk? The earth is charged with energy—electromagnetic energy. Our bodies actually become more stable, more balanced because of this connection to the Earth.

Have you ever felt a surge of energy after spending time in a bookstore or a library? Remember, those books were once trees and as far-fetched as that might seem, earth energy still exists in them. Perhaps an afternoon of connecting with a book is not a bad idea at all. Your awareness of your groundedness with the Earth is an important factor in your mental and physical health.

Negative thinking affects that health, and can cause serious health issues. Under constant stress, we gradually suppress our immune systems which can result in a variety of problems. We can be renewed and restored to health by simply grounding ourselves in the ever-present source of energy. Without the Earth, our energy becomes depleted because of our electromagnetic attraction to the Earth. It's a little like taking the phone off the charger. Without the connection again, the phone's energy is gone. Our energy—body, mind and spirit energy—is like that, too.

Perhaps that is the reason I felt so at home during my camping days at Winnetaska, and on camping trips with my family. We walked barefoot those days, always in touch with the ground or the water. Without this infinite source of energy which is connected to the Earth, we eventually deplete our energy mentally, physically and spiritually, and will find it difficult to move forward to achieve our dreams. We become tired, feel hopeless, fearful, fragmented, and disillusioned. Some of us might try to sustain our energy by using excessive mental effort, sugar, caffeine, or even drugs, however the resulting over-excited frenetic energy does not last and is, at best, only a short-term.

I am reminded of the words from James Weldon Johnson's sermon called "The Creation Story:"

Up from the bed of the river, God scooped the clay, and by the bank of the river he kneeled him down... and there the Great God Almighty, who lit the Sun and fixed it in the sky, who flung the starts to the far most corners of the night, who rounded the Earth in the palm of his hand… this Great God, like a mammy bending over her baby… kneeled down in the dust toiling over a lump of clay….till he shaped it in his own image. Then into it he breathed the breath of life, and man became a living soul.

We are a part of the Earth, the Earth is a part of us. No wonder it makes us feel so much at home.

As an exercise to feel your connection to the Earth, try this meditation called *The Tree of Life* from "The Spiral Dance" by Starhawk.

As you breathe, remember to sit erect, and as your spine straightens, feel the energy rising…(pause)

Now imagine your spine is the trunk of a tree…and from its base, roots extend deep into the earth…into the center of the earth, herself. (Pause)

And you can draw up power from the earth, with each breath…feel the energy rising…like sap rising through a tree trunk…and feel your roots intertwine with the roots of others, drawing energy together.

And feel the power rise up your spine…feel yourself becoming more alive with each breath.

And from the crown of your head, you have branches that sweep up and back down to touch the earth... and feel the power burst from the crown of your head and feel it sweep through the branches until it touches the earth again... making a circle...making a circuit...returning to its source...

And breathing deeply, feel how your branches intertwine with the branches of others... and the power weaves through them...and dances among them like the wind...

Now sink to the ground and relax. Place your palms flat on the ground...Let the power sink through you...let it flow back deeply into the earth where it will be cleansed and renewed.

Connections to Children

Never overlook the value of connecting with children. Children have a wonderful way of keeping you real, and keeping you honest with yourself. Oh, they can certainly tire you out, but there is nothing wrong with the good tiredness that comes from a time with children. I love the young children that I taught—their hunger for knowledge, their innate understanding of how to stretch the limits, their wonder and awe, and their joy of movement.

Connect with children and look for the things I mentioned above. You will learn as much from them as they learn from you. I long for those times that I had with my grandchildren when they were young. I was so very lucky to be close to them and experience many, many times together.

Now they are adults. Since I have retired from teach, my dance students no longer satisfy that longing to connect with children. The time has come to find some more children to stir the wonder and awe in me

I remember being nurtured by older people when I was a child, especially my grandparents. When I was young, my entire extended family live in Birmingham, AL. When we visited Birmingham, my favorite memory of all was going to the Alabama Theater to see Fred Astaire movies with my Grandmother. It was just our special thing to do. She loved the musicals with all the singing and dancing, and so did I. Maybe she knew, and maybe she never knew, that she was feeding my soul! Who knows? That may have been the beginning of this long dance career. Her inspiration became my inspiration.

Grandday told us stories of Scotland that nurtured my desire to travel.

What memories are you creating with children? What memories are you creating for children, and how will those memories influence their future? It is important to keep children a part of your life.

Connections with Animals

There is the obvious connection that we have to our pets. Most of us treat them and love them like humans. We can enjoy connections with other creatures, too. I have always been a little afraid of birds. I don't know why. For several summers I had the opportunity to really enjoy and get to know something about some birds. One day, I saw some birds busy going and coming and stopping in a corner in the eaves of my front porch. One beak full of mud at a time they were building a little round nest in the corner. They were quite the builders. They stacked those little muddy lumps exactly like bricks. It took them only a couple of days to complete the nest. I discovered that these birds are Barn Swallows.

Then not long afterward, the pair looked different to me. They seemed to be thin. I realized that they had lined the nest with their feathers. Not long after that, they began to take turns sitting on the nest. I must have spent hours just watching those birds. So did my cat. She sat right under them and watched them build. And then we saw five tiny heads with wide open mouths peek up out of the nest. Mother and Father birds took turns leaving the nest to return with food. The birds hardly seemed to notice the cat, Kaboodle, and me. They were busy. Three weeks later it was time for the baby birds to leave the nest—an unbelievably short time. One at a time, they jumped out of the nest and joined their parents in flight. It was amazing to watch. When all five were flying, they were often gone most of the day, but every evening for a few weeks, they returned to snuggle together on the ledge for the night.

Later, after they left, another pair came, spruced up the nest a bit, lined it with new feathers, and then the family came. This pair was noticeably different from the first. They were not quite so sure about our presence.

There were two pairs of birds every year after that. And, every pair had different personalities. I didn't know that about birds. Sometimes they easily accepted that Kaboodle and I were part of their chosen home. Other times, they were afraid of us. When the babies were ready to fly, sometimes they scared me by dive-bombing us as I left the house. Occasionally, I would even go out the back door to avoid them. That latent fear wasn't gone completely. I did have a new appreciation for, and a new connection to, birds.

I truly connected with those birds for many years. They were definitely a part of my life. I learned so much from them. Most of all, I learned that birds have personalities just like people. They help each other, they have fears, and they care for their young. The last year that I lived at the house, there were again five little birds in the nest. The parents had been a little later in building and nesting than in the past. All the Barn Swallows usually left the area at one time late in the summer. When that time came, my baby birds had not yet flown. As usual one by one, they joined their parents, that is, all except one. For a couple of days that baby would not leave the nest. I happened to be standing there when it happened. The mother bird, literally, kicked the baby out of the nest, and then she waited. Nothing happened, so she got close and nudged that baby off the ledge with a force to be reckoned with. The baby flew and joined the others as they left with the rest. No snuggling this time on the ledge at night. They were late to join the rest. I am not sure where they were going, but they connected with the others just in time.

Give some thought to how you connect with other people and with all other aspects of God's creation. What keeps you from being lonely? Do you have a diverse system of connections? It is very important to your well-being and your health. Be aware.

Value your connections

Chapter Ten
Celebratio and Conclusion

Timely Tip # 10   Make Every Day a Celebration Day

It is good to celebrate. When we celebrate, we appreciate.

I celebrate that I have been close to my grandchildren since they were born. I had many Celebration Days with Christian (Ki), and with Katherine *Kat). Celebrating life with grandchildren is always a treat. Can we make every day a celebration day by noticing those things around us that give us pleasure? The sun, the moon, the ants, the birds, the rocks are there for us to notice everyday, but we are often too busy to notice. Sometimes as I read the Facebook posts of many friends, it looks as if they are lamenting rather than celebrating. Perhaps we would recognize the joys of life more if we could find something to celebrate each day.

I wrote a Celebration Story by combining many days that Kit and I spent together. I share it with you here as an example of how you might write about your own Celebration Day.

Celebration Day

"Dear Kit,

You are invited…

To a Celebration Day!

Love,

Nana"

"Good Morning, Kit."

"Good Morning, Nana. Good Morning, Mr. Sun. Nana open the curtains so I can see the sun!"

"It's a beautiful wonderful day, Kit. What shall we do today?" Kit and I have the whole week together. We have plans to make. Kit is two years old and I am sixty-two. He is my precious grandson and I see my role in his life as one of celebration—celebration of living together in this universe on this planet called Earth. This day, like all other days, is a day to celebrate, to give thanks and to participate in our small, but wonderful, part of the Universe Story.

As I read the words of Thomas Berry commenting on a book of verse for children, it seems as though they were written for me.

It takes a universe to make a child both in outer form and inner spirit. It takes a universe to educate a child.

Each generation presides over the meeting of these Two in the succeeding generation.

So now we write our own verses bringing the child and universe into their mutual fulfillment.

While the stars ring out in the heavens. Thomas Berry

At this moment in my life, nothing is more important to me than handing down the story of the universe to my grandchildren. You might say that it is my present way of contributing to sustainability. Can my stories and poems and games with a small child truly contribute to this process? I think the lines above from Thomas Berry support my thesis that any way we can help children to be aware of their cosmology, root them in universe stories, and leave them hungry for more stories and for their own exploration, does indeed, contribute towards the sustainability of the universe. So, let's get on with Kit and Nana's Celebration Day. All of these events have actually taken place for Kit and me. Every day that we play together is a celebration day,

"What's that sound, Nana?"

"I hear a bird singing Kit. But wait, I hear another sound. Is that baby birds I hear?"

"Let's go see! Let's go see! We run to the window and sure enough, the nest we've been watching for several days has four new baby birds. All we can really see is four wide open mouths.

"Why are they opening their mouths like that, Nana?" "Because they are hungry. They want Mommy Bird to feed them. Are you hungry, too? Let's go and find you some breakfast." As I prepare his cinnamon toast, he watches the birds and finds it hard to pull himself away when his breakfast is ready. He climbs into his high chair and opens his mouth wide. We both laugh as I drop in a piece of toast.

Breakfast over, Kit is excited to take a morning walk. We like to walk early in the morning to see who else is awake. The ants are always awake and very busy. They live in the cracks in the sidewalk and Kit is careful not to step on them. We watch them carry things bigger than themselves. Such fascinating activity! Then Kit's eyes are drawn to a yellow butterfly. He watches as it dances in the sky and then, joined by another, flutters about amongst the flowers. Kit stretches out his arms like butterfly wings and dances happily across the grass.

On this morning walk we notice a Mourning Dove, a caterpillar, a bee, beautiful flowers and clouds in the sky— today they are puffy and white in a bright blue sky. The Mourning Dove reminds me of my mother who always loved their sound. On the day we buried her, one came and sat quietly by her grave. As we walked away, it cooed its mournful tune and I knew Mom had a new place in the universe. I told Kit that morning a little about his great grandmother. I wish he could have known her.

Each creature we met had its own story to tell. We talked with wonder about how the caterpillar might soon become a butterfly. Kit's face looked a bit mystified as he considered the possibility. He looked first at the caterpillar and then at the butterfly fluttering nearby. "What will I become, Nana?" he asked with a little concern on his face.

"You'll become a man, Kit…first, a big boy and then a man."

" Oh! A big boy like William and a man like Daddy?"

"That's right!" He seems satisfied with that becoming and we continued along on our walk.

Our morning walks bring new sights and sounds. Kit's not fond of bees—one stung him on the neck. He shows them great respect saying, "Go away please, Mr. Bee." It is not hard for me to notice the kinship he senses for all the natural things we see.

"Let's go to the park, Nana. I want to slide." We drive to a park that I particularly like because the rocks and trees weren't cleared in order to put up the playground equipment. Kit joyfully slides on all the various sizes of slides that the park engineers have planned. He goes through the tunnels, up and down and then, he tires of that and turns to climbing the rocks.

"Look, Nana I'm on the mountain! Find me Nana. I'm behind the big tree!" He picks up pine cones finding some that the squirrels have eaten. He looks for squirrels in the trees and wishes he could climb like Mr. Squirrel. He spends much more time on the natural playground than on the plastic one.

Finally, he tires of that, too. It almost lunch time and nap time (Whew!). I sit down beside him on a huge rock. He snuggles up beside me and says, "Tell me a story."

"Oh Kit, listen—the rock we're sitting on is telling you a story. He squeezes a little closer, listening to the rock...

The Rock's Story

Once a long, long time ago, I lived in this place all alone. No trees live here. No plants or animals lived here. I was all alone except for the warm sun I felt in the morning and the cool breeze that I felt in the evening. During the day, I could see the clouds as they floated through the sky, and at night I saw the stars as they twinkled so far away. Sometimes I felt raindrops and occasionally a few snowflakes rested on shoulders. Other than that, there was nothing more to feel.

One day I saw something very strange. It was little creature with wings. I asked, "Who are you?" "I am a bird," it said. Well, Kit I can tell you that I was very happy to see this bird. I had been lonely for a long time. I asked her if she could stay with me. She looked around and said that she could not stay because there was nothing here for her to eat and drink. When I waved good-bye to her, I was very sad. Inside me, my heart broke just a little bit. Tears came from deep inside and made a little stream. The next time the bird flew by, she dropped something from her beak. I know now that it was a little seed. After that, I noticed that something strange was happening to me. Right beside the stream of tears there was a softer spot on me. Suddenly a little leaf poked its head right out of my side. Changes began to happen all around me. Trees grew and as they grew, insects came and then animals came. I looked and looked for my special friend and then, one day she came. She built a nest here in the tree right beside you. Oh Kit it made me so happy! Now I'm not lonely anymore. And today, I'm even happier because you've come to play. Thanks for climbing on my shoulders today. And oh by the way, take care of all my friends,

"Time to say good-bye to the rock, Kit."

"Bye-bye, Mr. Rock. I'll come back to see you." By the time we get home, Kit is sound asleep. I tuck him into his bed and wonder about his dreams. Is he dreaming about the rock that loved a little bird?

When he wakes up after his nap, it's time for dinner. After dinner we decide to take a "dark walk." Kit is just a little afraid of the dark. "Will you hold me, Nana?"

"Yes, I'll hold you. Let's go look for the moon." With that he is ready. He's had a special relationship with the moon since he was 9 months old. The first time I held him up to look at the moon, he shivered with delight. I said, "That's the moon, Kit. Can you say moon?"

"Moooooon!" he said with obvious fascination.

Tonight the moon is almost full, but it is a cloudy night. "Where are you Mr. Moon? Are you hiding in the trees?" And then we see it, peeking out from the clouds. He squeals and says, "Hold me up, Nana, so I can touch the moon."

"Oh Kit. I can't hold you that high."

"Then maybe someday, I'll be an astronaut so I can play with the moon." (Now where did he learn that)?

We didn't see many stars that night, but sang "Twinkle, Twinkle Little Star" anyway.

After a day of celebration, this Nana is tired, too.

"Good night, Kit."

"Good night, Nana. Sweet dreams, Mr. Moon!"

Just as an exercise, write a celebration day story about your day today. Would it change your outlook on your life if you found everyday things to celebrate? Would a sense of gratitude and appreciation chance how you feel mentally and emotionally?

When I started to write this book, I thought it was a book for "older adults." But, when is it that people start to think of themselves as old. I hear people start calling themselves old at forty, or when they notice the first wrinkle.

That state of mind we call young is not a matter of rosy cheeks, and joints that don't crackle and pop; it is a matter of choice, of rich imagination, vitality of the emotions; it is the celebration of life itself.

Aging well means acting out of courage over timidity. It means having an appetite for adventure over the love of ease. Nobody grows old merely by a number of years. We grow old by deserting our ideals, our dreams, and our goals.

"Years may wrinkle the skin, but to give up enthusiasm wrinkles the soul. Worry, fear, self-distrust bows the heart and turns the spirit back to dust."

We are lured by wonder, joy of life, and childlike appetite for what's next, whether we are ninety or nineteen. In the center of your heart and my heart there is a spirit receiving your messages of beauty, hope, cheer, courage, and power, as long as your mind accepts the messages.

When your spirit is covered with snows of cynicism and the ice of pessimism, then you have grown old, even at twenty. As long as you choose to catch the waves of optimism, there is hope that you will stay forever young.

Something that almost always accompanies celebration is laughter. Humor is infectious. The sound of roaring laughter is highly contagious. The giggle of a baby is a most wonderful sound. When laughter is shared, it binds people together and increases happiness and intimacy. In addition to the domino effect of joy and amusement, laughter also triggers healthy physical changes in the body. Humor and laughter strengthen your immune system, boost your energy, diminish pain, and protect you from the damaging effects of stress. Best of all, this priceless medicine is fun, free, and easy to use. It has been said that laughter is interior jogging. Choose laughter.

Ways to help yourself see the lighter side of life:

- Surround yourself with reminders to lighten up. Keep a toy on your couch or in your car. Put up a funny poster in your kitchen. Frame photos of you and you family or friends having fun.

- Keep things in perspective. Many things in life are beyond our control—particularly the behavior of other people. While you might think taking the weight of the world on your shoulders is admirable, in the long run it's unrealistic, unproductive, unhealthy, and even egotistical.

- Deal with your stress. Stress is a major impediment to humor and laughter.

- Pay attention to children and emulate them. They are the experts on playing, taking life lightly, and laughter.

Do you move boldly into the party of life, or do you hold back? Being involved in the party, in the celebration, plays an important role in improving self-esteem and giving meaning to life. This is true for people of all ages, but is especially important for older adults. What ways can you find to celebrate today?

***Make every day a Celebration Day*splashes

Conclusion… What's next?

I will close with a song by Sleeping at Last…I could call it "My Song."

How nice it'd be
If we could try everything
I'm serious, let's make a list and just begin
What about danger?
So what?
What about risk?
Let's climb this mountain before we cross that bridge!

'Cause I'm restless
I'm restless
I'm restless
For whatever comes next

How wonderful to see a smile on your face
It costs farewell tears for a welcome-home parade
A secret handshake between me and my one life
I'll find the silver lining, no matter what the price

'Cause I'm hungry
Oh, I'm hungry
I'm hungry
For whatever comes next

Let me tell you another secret of the trade
It feels like sinking when I'm standing in one place

So I look to the future
And I book another flight
When everything feels heavy, I've learned to travel light

But I want to be here
Truly be here
To watch the ones that I love bloom
And I want to make room
To love them through, and through, and through, and through
The slow and barren seasons, too

I feel hope
Deep in my bones
Tomorrow will be beautiful

And I'm ready
God, I'm ready
Oh, I'm ready
Restless and hungry!
I'm ready for whatever comes next

Live a purpose-filled life enjoying the challenges of goals and dreams. Take care of your body and your mind simply by using them. Let your spirit soar releasing your soul. Search your heart and listen to its longings. Rejoice in your connection with all of Creation, and celebrate every day!

What's Next?

Appendix:

Meditation Stretch

Let's do a stretching meditation to ready your body for movement. You might want to copy the words in bold type and put them where you read as you go through the movements. Even better, you could record them leaving time for the movement in between the reading.

These simple movements are to be done very slowly and with reverence. This is an invitation to God, to Spirit, and to community. It gives recognition to our connection to all life — life that has gone before us and life that is to come.

The stretch can be done with any slow, peaceful music, a steady drum beat, or with no music at all, just your inner rhythm. Or, engage the YouTube link that will give you music and narration. I enjoy the Native American feeling of this meditation and like to use a drum beat to accompany the movements.

In silence light a candle. Then stand facing front to begin.

Narration: *I am a part of a vast web of life. I stand between our ancestors and our descendants. I ask for blessings of peace and healing for all people.*

Honor the four directions: north, east, south and west, recognizing that we are all one, offering light to the

world. Slowly move the candle forward stretching your arms in front of you, then bring it back in toward your heart, stretch arms up connecting to God, and back into your heart, then reaching forward again, turn one-quarter turn toward the side. Continue through all directions. Place the candle on the floor in front of you.

Narration: *The space has been cleared, the offering has been made, I am open to receive.*

The rhythm has begun, I leave the past behind and enter the sacred…

Sit down on a chair or the floor. Sit tall, then slowly bend forward moving your head toward your toes, return to sitting slowly. Repeat this movement twice.

Now, slowly move through gestures of petition (like praying hands), reach (reaching upward), receive (cup hands like you are receiving a gift), and share (open arms like you are sharing the gift you receive) Repeat this two times.

Return to forward stretch, repeating it twice.

Narration: *Hear me, Most Sacred! The Power that moves everything told me the great Vision: to give birth to a good power of the inner spirit. Thank you, all my Relations, all over the universe. I am saying this.*

Stand

Reach arms high and bend forward slowly.

Reach arms up again and then open them slowly to the side.

Repeat.

Reach one arm to the side, then stretch overhead and bend to the side. Repeat this pattern lifting the other arm.

Repeat slowly facing each direction (do this four times in all).

Sit down and sit quietly for a few moments.

Narration: *My spirits is renewed, my heart are open, I am at peace.*

As you finish your warm-up stretch and meditation, explore the season you have chosen with one of the suggested meditations or one that you create for yourself.

Create Your Dance

Different ways of combining and using these elements determine the expression of your dance, just as re-ordering words in a sentence changes the meaning of the sentence.

Dynamics describe how the body moves.

- Duration – the length of time needed to do a movement…short or long.

- Energy – the muscular tension used to move…a little or a lot

- Rhythm – Even rhythm – a steady equal rhythm or, an uneven rhythm

- Quality – characteristics of a movement; for example, strong or light

- Speed – fast or slow

Actions are what the body is doing. By finding out, through movement explorations, what your body can do and by expanding your body's abilities, you can build a repertoire of movements that we might use in a dance or in life. This is called a movement vocabulary. A rich movement vocabulary increases the capacity to express ourselves.

Actions can travel (locomotor) or move on the spot (axial). They fall into the following categories; traveling, stillness, gesturing, jumping, falling, turning, twisting, contracting, expanding and transferring weight.

Create an action word list for yourself of actions that you can do. These action words will become your dance steps. Out of these natural movements you will create your dance.

The body is the instrument of dance. Just as a painter paints with a brush, in dance it is through the body that the picture appears. We can enjoy the body and its potential for movement. As we age, we will adjust what we expect our bodies to do. Try to incorporate your whole body as you dance. Use this as a guide:

Body parts – head, arms, hands, legs, feet, torso, elbows, wrists, shoulders, hips, knees, ankles

Body zones – body areas of front, back, left side, right side, upper half, lower half

Body bases – whatever supports the rest of the body; for example, when standing—the feet, when kneeling—the knees.

A dancer will explore and use a variety of whole body and body part actions, body bases and body zones in their dance experiences.

The relationships in your dance may be described as the correspondence or connection between things, be they dancers to each other, dancers to objects or a dancer's body parts to each other. Explore the relationships of connecting, leading, following, meeting, parting, near, far, passing by and surrounding.

We use space when we dance. Space is where the body moves. As dancers move through space, their bodies create patterns on the floor and in the air. These designs or patterns are an integral part of dance. You might choose to use both general space (the area you have available in which to dance, or you may choose to use your personal space, the space you can reach while staying in place.

Other ingredients for your dance may include:

Directions – forward, backward, sideways, diagonal, upward or downward

Focus – where the eyes or the intention of the movement is directed

Levels – high, middle and low or deep

Pathways – the patterns or designs made in the air or on the floor by the person's movements; pathways appear as straight lines, curved lines or combinations of straight and curved lines

Shape – the design of the body's position

Size – the magnitude of the body shape or movement; size is on a continuum of small to large.

Enjoy creating your story/dance. You can use the ideas above, or just let the movement flow from your natural movement vocabulary.

Good nutrition leads to endurance

"Let us run with endurance the race that is set before us."

Hebrews 12:1

- Would you trust your body to take you on a long-distance trek in an emergency?

- If you had to count on your body to save a loved one who needed you to be physically strong, would you be able to?

- If you had to run away to escape danger, could you?

These questions were asked by Dr. Erik Plasker in his book called "The 100 Year Lifestyle." Ponder them for a few minutes. Your endurance is important. With high endurance, you can enjoy a great sense of stamina and activity while you age. Your energy will be high and you will feel like doing things. You can increase your stamina and endurance through daily cardiovascular exercise that strengthens your heart, burns calories, and increases your energy. Find ways that you enjoy to increase your cardiovascular activity over the next few months. Dr. Plasker suggests a 10% increase each month for three months. That is possible. Have fun doing things that make you feel strong and vibrant every day.

Last week I heard an interview with a man who was 104. When asked what he thought he did that contributed to his longevity he answered, "Dance, laugh, and love the ladies." I like that answer. Move vigorously to music and rhythm, have fun, and stay connected to others you enjoy.

Resources:

Chapter One:

Fox, Matthew (1994). Reinvention of work: a new vision of livelihood for our time. HarperSanFrancisco.

Gladstone, J. W. (1992) The builders. On Buckskin poet society.

Columbiana Falls, Mt.: Sight and Sound Studios, and Seattle, WA: MacDonald Recording.

Helliwell, Tanis (1997). Summer with the leprechauns: a true story. Nevada City, CA: Blue Dolphin Publishing

Helliwell, Tanis (1999). Take your soul to work: transform your life and work. Holbrook, Massachusetts: Adams Media Corporation.

Suzuki, David (1997,2002). The sacred balance: rediscovering our place in nature. Vancouver, British Columbia: Greystone Books.

Chapter Four:

ACE Personal Trainer Manual, Third Edition, Copyright 2003, 1196 American Council on Exercise, page 23

Sarcopenia: The Mystery of Muscle Loss, Chantal Vella, M.S. and Len Kravitz, Ph.D.

Chapter Seven:

Chanda, Mona Lisa, and Daniel J. Levitin. "The neurochemistry of music." *Trends in cognitive sciences* 17.4 (2013): 179-193

Kweh, Birgit. "Dance as therapy: An investigation of available evidence in the field of Dance/Movement Therapy, and plausible mechanisms behind potential effects." (2011).

How Arts Training Improves Attention and Cognition. The Dana Foundation, September 14, 2009.

Verghese, Joe, et al. "Leisure activities and the risk of dementia in the elderly." New England Journal of Medicine 348.25 (2003): 2508-2516.

Alves, Heloisa. Dancing and the aging brain: the effects of a 4-month ballroom dance intervention on the cognition of healthy older adults. Diss. University of Illinois at Urbana-Champaign, 2013.

Sandel, Susan L., et al. "Dance and Movement Program Improves Quality-

Chapter Eight:

Cendrars, Blaise (1982) *Shadow* (Marcia Brown, Trans.) New York: Charles Scribner's Sons.

Swimme, Brian (1996). *The Hidden Heart of the Cosmos: Humanity and the New Story*. Maryknoll, New York: Orbis Books

Chapter Nine:

Yeh, 2000, as cited in New Village Journal ¶

Heart Association, 1995, p. 21-22)

Heather Winkle, Vice President of Design, Capital One

Chapter Ten:

The Tree of Life from "The Spiral Dance" by Starhawk

The Mountain That Loved a Bird by Alice McLerran (The Rock's story is a paraphrase of this beautiful book).

Sleeping at Last is a musical project led by singer-songwriter and multi-instrumentalist Ryan O'Neal. The project initially began in Wheaton, Illinois as a three-piece band with Ryan O'Neal as the lead singer and guitarist, his brother Chad O'Neal as the drummer, and Dan Perdue as the bassist.

Made in the USA
Columbia, SC
26 September 2024